Damn Good Food

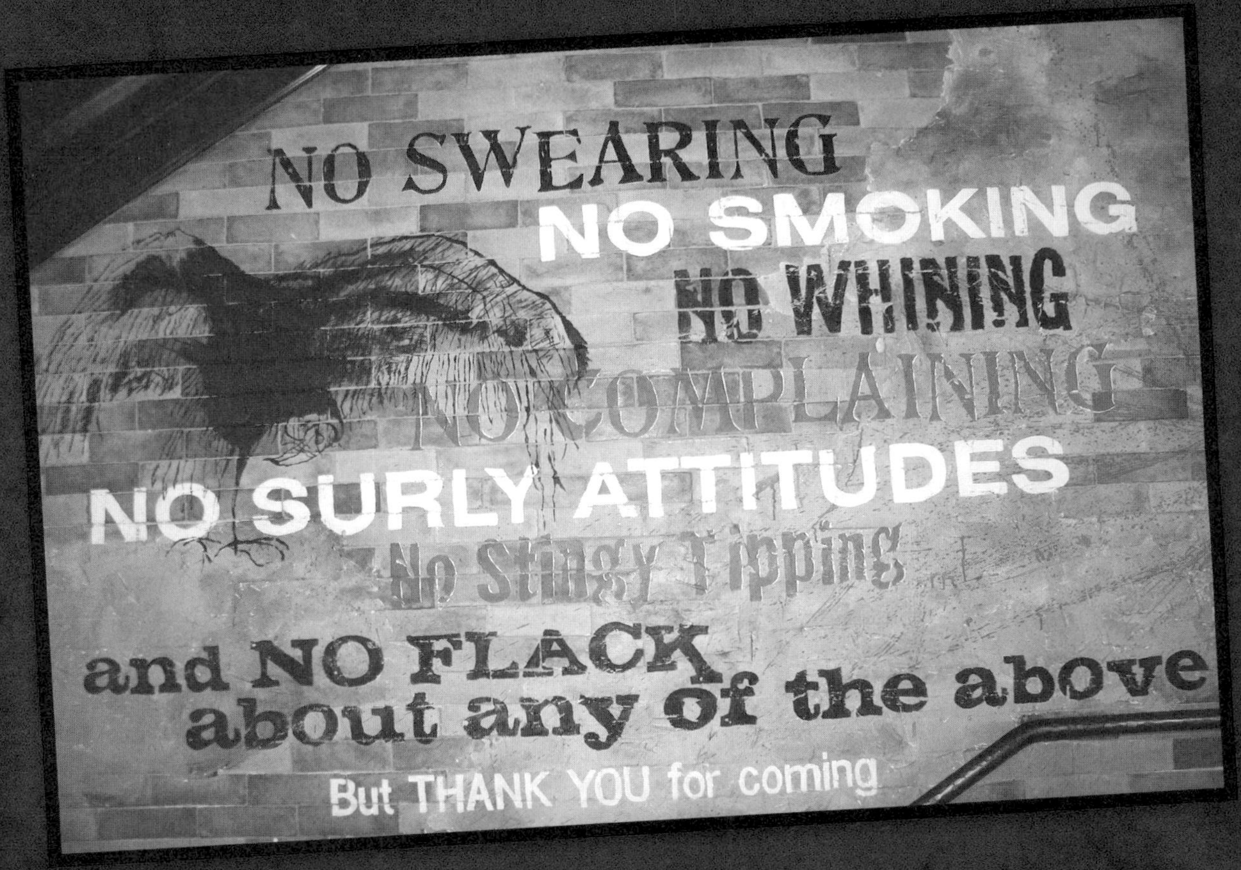
NO SWEARING
NO SMOKING
NO WHINING
NO COMPLAINING
NO SURLY ATTITUDES
No Stingy Tipping
and NO FLACK
about any of the above
But THANK YOU for coming

DAMN GOOD FOOD

157 Recipes from HELL'S KITCHEN

MITCH OMER AND ANN BAUER

BOREALIS
BOOKS

Borealis Books is an imprint of the Minnesota Historical Society Press.

www.borealisbooks.org

Cover photography: Dolce Studios
Cover design: Percolator

The Minnesota Historical Society Press is a member
of the Association of American University Presses.

Manufactured in Canada

10 9 8 7 6 5 4 3 2 1

♾ The paper used in this publication meets the minimum requirements of the American National Standard for Information Sciences—Permanence for Printed Library Materials, ANSI Z39.48–1984.

International Standard Book Number
ISBN-13: 978-0-87351-724-9 (cloth)
ISBN-10: 0-87351-724-5 (cloth)

Library of Congress Cataloging-in-Publication Data

Omer, Mitch, 1954–
    Damn good food : 157 recipes from Hell's Kitchen / Mitch Omer and Ann Bauer.
        p. cm.
    Includes bibliographical references and index.
    ISBN-13: 978-0-87351-724-9 (cloth : alk. paper)
    ISBN-10: 0-87351-724-5 (cloth : alk. paper)
    1. Cookery, American. 2. Hell's Kitchen (Restaurant : Minneapolis, Minn.)
3. Omer, Mitch, 1954– I. Bauer, Ann. II. Hell's Kitchen (Restaurant : Minneapolis, Minn.)
III. Title.
    TX715.O51245 2009
    641.5973—dc22   2009024491

To Dana and Annie Omer (inspirations inside the kitchen and out) and Aunt Frances (Patron Saint of Lost Nephews)

Contents

3 Introduction

9 Hearth and Home: Recipes from the Heartland

33 Drugs, Sex, and Gluttony: Recipes from the Vagabond Years

49 Manic Cuisine: Recipes from Hell's Kitchen

57 Breakfast and Brunch

97 Sandwiches and Burgers

125 Entrées

141 Condiments, Spices, and Sauces

161 Baked Goods

171 Libations: Spicy, Cold, and Hot

179 Cuisine Savage: Recipes for Wild Game and Quarry

197 Sacred Rites: Recipes for Funerals, Weddings, and New Year's Day

207 Index

DAMN GOOD FOOD

INTRODUCTION

It was a chilly autumn morning in 2004. I was the food editor at a Minneapolis lifestyle magazine with six pages to fill in an upcoming issue but no ideas. Then my phone rang. A woman told me that she and her husband had a restaurant named Hell's Kitchen and he'd recently auditioned for a reality show with the same name. But he didn't make the cut.

"So what's the story?" I asked.

"Come meet him," she said, laughing. "See for yourself."

I was desperate. Plus, Hell's Kitchen was only two blocks from my office—in a crooked, crumbling little alley of a building, between an appliance store and a wig shop. So on a whim I grabbed my notebook and pen, walked over, and pushed my way through a heavy wrought-iron gate.

Inside, the restaurant was a blood red cave with black linens and Ralph Steadman paintings—leering monsters in bright clothes, like the nightmare side of *Sesame Street*—lining the walls. I felt as if I'd entered some secret, private club: there were men in three-piece suits with ties thrown over their shoulders forking up enormous bites of *huevos rancheros*; well-coiffed businesswomen snatched at buttered sausage bread and sweet potato fries with their perfectly manicured hands.

I asked for the owner, and a hulking man came stumping out of a back room with a five-foot walking stick. Both his legs were working just fine, so I couldn't figure out the huge stick. What's more, he did *not* look happy to see me. This guy had wild, white hair that flared to one side as if he were standing in the wind. His face was creased; his wire rim glasses, askew. I strongly suspected he'd been sleeping in back. But before I could back out the door, he barked at me to sit down.

I did so and then asked him about the show. "I *hate* fucking reality TV!" he cried out in a voice as deep and nasal as a bassoon. The few people who were eating breakfast turned to look. "But I heard about this goddamn show doing tryouts, and I have proprietary rights over the name Hell's Kitchen here in Minneapolis. So I started making phone calls."

Then he found out the show would award a fully equipped high-end Los Angeles restaurant to the winner. So he went to the casting call instead. There, he completed a videotaped interview and filled out a twenty-five-page background application that asked him to list every romantic relationship he'd ever had. That took *lots* of extra paper, he said, raising one crooked eyebrow, and the better part of a day.

But in the end no one from Fox TV called.

"They probably thought I was too old, which is shit," he said, leaning forward. "But I think I had about a dozen other factors working against me, too, not the least of which is my foul language. And I probably shouldn't have told them I'm bipolar or obsessive-compulsive or that I was in treatment last year. I said that I own handguns. They asked if I'd ever been in jail, and I said, 'Yes, I have, actually.' A studio executive sees someone with my profile, he might think I'm a risk."

I looked up to see if he was joking. His blue eyes were as clear as a baby's.

"Hey, you want something to eat?" he asked.

I shook my head. "I've already had . . ."

But this guy was paying no attention. He stood, towering over me, and beckoned a young man whose lips were studded with bolts. "Get her some Mahnomin porridge," he barked, then turned back to me. "You'll love this; it's my own recipe."

Five minutes later, a bowl the circumference of a Frisbee arrived, and inside was a colorful, steaming stew of wild rice, roasted hazelnuts, and dried blueberries and cranberries. I took a tiny spoonful, and the taste was of nutty popcorn, sunlight, blueberry pie, and chewy fruit-cake—all swimming in heavy, maple-spiked cream.

I ate the entire thing.

BACK THEN, I WAS STRUGGLING with a conundrum. At least four times a week, someone told me I had their dream job. And I knew I should agree: when I was offered the position, that's exactly how I'd imagined I would feel.

But in reality I was angry, isolated, lonely, and bored.

This isn't something you're allowed to say out loud. A food critic is supposed to act humbly grateful: demure about all the luscious meals she is fed, willing to debate favorite restaurants with everyone she meets. No one sees that you actually spend your life assembling dinner parties by rounding up compatible friends—like some perpetual junior high school test—or that you need a graphing calculator to count the calories you consume. You skip these parts and perpetuate the myth, letting people think you have a fabulous merry-go-round of a life.

But here's the truth: fine dining can be stultifying—all dripping ice sculptures and handsome Ken doll chefs, with their weirdly anorectic supermodel girlfriends, and applause all around the table every time a server sets down a vertically sculpted dish.

Ramps were all the rage in 2004. So was lamb. I ate ramps and lamb, lamb with ramps. Nearly every chef I spoke to acted as if he'd invented them both. What's more, I saw the same thirty or so people nearly every night. This was Minneapolis, after all, not San Francisco or Chicago. We had a small group of foodies that followed new restaurant openings cultishly, talking about the chefs in hushed tones, using their first names as if they were very close friends. Only no one was. The discussion over dinner was rarely personal; no one knew the names of each other's children or political leanings. The only real topic of interest was food.

By late 2004 I'd lost my hunger, and I mean that in every way. I'd been single for three years at this point and celibate for nearly two. Dating seemed redundant. Men would take me to the places I visited for work, and I would sit all evening, toying with my deconstructed food, making small talk, wishing I were home alone under a blanket watching *Law & Order*. Finally, I just quit trying. My senses were dull.

Then I stumbled across Mitch Omer; his wife, Cynthia; and his parents, Dana and Annie. We sat around crowded tables where the conversation ranged from cosmology to travel to art. I ate fresh homemade peanut butter straight out of the giant mixer, ham and pear sandwiches melty with fontina cheese, bison sausage cooked in butter and black coffee. I fell recklessly in love with a motorcycle racer, whom I met—and married—in the company of these people.

In short, everything changed.

MITCH OMER IS INSANE, and I mean that in the best—but also the most literal—way.

By the time he was ten, his parents knew something was wrong. They took him to psychologists, but no one could pinpoint the problem. He was impulsive. He set fires and got into fights. He was smart but never did well in school.

By his twenties this six-foot-five-inch guy was rocketing around the world getting jobs and losing them; working as a bodyguard for rock bands, marrying women and leaving them; brawling, drinking, drugging, and running up bills for things he didn't need.

He spent his thirties moving from one itinerant cooking post to another. His talent in the kitchen was obvious—it was as if he could feel the way food should taste—and that carried him a long way. But eventually, inevitably, he'd be fired for excessive profanity, insubordination, or sleeping with the boss's wife. Often he'd get frustrated and simply walk out.

Most of this time was spent in Minneapolis, but Mitch also wandered out West—eventually going as far as California—learning the beer trade, cooking on hot lines, and nailing every woman who would have him, including one inside the industrial-size mash tun of the Colorado brewpub where he worked.

In the midnineties, however, Mitch hit bottom. Tired, depressed, bankrupt, and obese, he went into hiding in a remote northern Minnesota town called Ely where his family had vacationed when he was a child. At his heaviest he weighed more than four hundred pounds. For five years no woman would touch him. The only sensual pleasures left to him were food, drink, and the occasional sauna. His midlife crisis was epic. Shortly after turning forty, Mitch quit going out in public, neglecting the eleven-year-old son who lived with him and twice contemplating suicide.

He told me all this that first day, over my empty bowl, as we sat in Hell's Kitchen.

"How did you get from there to here?" I asked.

He rubbed his face, ran his fingers through his wild hair, and grinned. "I've got no goddamn idea," he said. "But I feel like the luckiest guy in the world."

The real answer is more complicated and less lyrical. He found a psychiatrist who diagnosed him at age forty-four with bipolar disorder and started him on psychiatric drugs. He underwent gastric bypass surgery and lost more than 165 pounds. Then, feeling good for the first time in years, he found a chef job at a small riverfront inn in St. Paul.

In 2000, his mother convinced him to sign up for an on-line dating service. He did so, and the following day he met Cynthia Gerdes, a Minneapolis businesswoman—owner of a $10 million toy company—and they have not been apart since. They married quickly and came up with the concept for Hell's Kitchen together, opening their doors in 2002.

By the time I walked in, two years later, the restaurant was already a local favorite. I wrote a feature about Mitch and Hell's Kitchen that caught the attention of local radio chef Lynne Rossetto Kasper and, in turn, Roadfood.com critics Jane and Michael Stern. They told the world that Hell's Kitchen makes "the best peanut butter we have ever sampled, anywhere." Internet orders poured in. Mitch opened a second location in northern Minnesota in 2007, and in 2008 he and Cynthia moved the original Hell's Kitchen to a prime 8,000-square-foot space in downtown Minneapolis.

But it doesn't matter how many tables they add. People are still lined up out the door.

Mitch makes extraordinary food. But even more important, from my perspective, he makes extraordinary *life*. And he knows what one has to do with the other—how food is only part of the equation. This is a man who wakes up every day full of gale-force curiosity and joy.

What's remarkable is that this is true no matter what his circumstances. Things aren't easy for Mitch. Because of his meds, he shakes so badly for the first couple hours of each day that he can barely hold a cup of coffee. The gastric bypass surgery makes it difficult for him to eat. We had to schedule work on this book around his second round in rehab and a court-ordered stint for driving under the influence, which he served in a Pine City, Minnesota, jail.

He's a hunter who can't steady a shotgun, an award-winning chef who can't eat a bite of rare steak, a lusty lifelong gourmet who cannot drink a glass of wine without risking his sobriety and his sanity. Fact is, they're teetering anyway. Debauchery and mania are the ghosts of his past, but they're also, always, around every bend. Yet Mitch forges ahead, a scholar, a minister, a sailor, and a musician. He's a diehard fan of Leonardo da Vinci. He's an artist, a voracious reader, a genuine tattoo freak. Food is his religion, but so too is astronomy, history, psychology, and botany. The outdoors. Family. Sex.

And despite everything that's happened, he still feels like the luckiest man alive.

"I wouldn't trade my life with anybody," Mitch will say. "I defy any person to say they've had a better experience than I have."

And it's true. Only, the remarkable thing is that when you're hanging out with Mitch Omer—eating his food and listening to his rumbling, braying belly laugh—it's true for you, too.

HEARTH and HOME

Des Moines isn't exactly in the top ten culinary destinations. But you wouldn't know that to hear Mitch talk.

He's as proud of his upbringing as he would be if he grew up in Chicago or New Orleans or Paris. And he recalls the delicacies from his childhood—fried sausage, waffles with home-made simple syrup, chicken and noodles served over mashed potatoes—the way another chef might talk about the local sweetbreads or chicory coffee and beignets. Mitch grew up eating pure comfort food, those roasting, crackling meals that smell like home on a cold winter evening. And this cuisine is at the base of everything he cooks at Hell's Kitchen today.

He was born in 1954, the middle child of Dana and Annie Omer, a telephone company worker and a nurse who'd been in love since the tenth grade. It doesn't get any more quaintly midwestern than this. The Omers lived in one of those cul-de-sac-filled suburban developments of ranch houses populated with people who looked just like them: young white couples with two or three children. Hibachis on the back deck and a blow-up swimming pool in every yard.

On weekends the entire neighborhood would gather at someone's house. The adults got schnockered on vodka tonics and sherry. They served salty, bite-sized things made from bottled and canned foods: baked chile squares, ham balls, Triscuits with Day-Glo spray cheese. The kids ran wild, finding empty bedrooms in which to experiment. "Four of those daughters

Annie and Dana Omer, 1970s style

ended up being my girlfriends," Mitch says. "Our parents never knew."

He and his older brother, Mark, were charming and handsome but troublesome kids. They set fires, including one that burned down a nearby garage. They roped their little sister, Libby, into helping them flood a neighbor's car by sticking a hose in the driver's door, shutting it, and turning the water on. Their parents vacillated between amusement and frustration. They tried punishing; they tried indulging; they tried taking the boys to therapy. But nothing really worked. Truth: it was an Omer family trait not to care what other people think.

Annie Omer was an adventurous cook but not necessarily a good one. She'd make last-minute substitutions: cornstarch for flour, hamburger for Italian sausage. A product of her time, she was constantly clipping magazine recipes, experimenting with canned soup, scanning Julia Child, and whipping up her own condiments. Her standard meals, such as a *Better Homes & Gardens*–style chicken divan, were great; others were hit-or-miss.

By Mitch's already hedonistic standards, his Aunt Fran was a phenomenal cook. She made things buttery, meaty, and sweet, with an utter disregard for nutrition. Cookies, bowls of candy, smoked and salted ham. Her pièce de résistance was chicken and homemade egg noodles atop mounds of mashed potatoes, a dish about which Mitch still dreams. It was an orgy of meat, schmaltz, and starch.

Fran was Annie's only sister. She lived two blocks away, and Mitch adored her, though the two women were often on the outs. Fiery and quick to take offense, Fran married five times—

four times to the same rough, profane man, the love of her life, Bud. Mitch hung out with his on-and-off uncle, who smoked and swore and kept a boat that he loved and waxed and stroked like the hood of a Rolls Royce. Four decades later, it's clear this is the man Mitch emulates, more even than the father he revered.

Bud and Fran: the fourth time's the charm

Back then, Dana was a pretty traditional weekend father and breakfast cook. He made cornmeal mush and white rice with raisins and cream. But his specialty was caramel rolls—a recipe based on the ones at Wall Drug in South Dakota but tinkered with for years until just right. That meant both sweet and rich (Dana was, says Annie, the only person she ever saw *butter* his cake), about a quarter pound each, as round as a saucer, and soft.

The Omers' favorite place to eat—considered exotic by Iowa standards—was the Sicilian section of Des Moines, where first-generation deli owners served what Dana called "guinea grinders": hot Italian sausage topped with banana peppers that they sizzled in the leftover grease before serving. On special occasions at home, Annie would make goulash and Dana would contribute a batch of his homemade coleslaw, which required a precise balance of garlic and cayenne.

The Omer family moved from Des Moines to Minneapolis in the early seventies. They loved the city: the nightlife, theaters, and restaurants. But they also missed their friends and drove back to Iowa several times a year to party with their old crowd.

There were only four of them by this time. Mark had married at seventeen, moved to Seattle, and was living under an assumed name to avoid the draft, which had caused a rift. Dana no longer spoke to Mark, and the family was at odds. Mitch and Libby attended a suburban Minneapolis high school. Both were tall and striking, like their mother. Despite this, Libby never dated in high school—not once—because all the boys in her class were terrified of her older brother. A star athlete with a growing tendency to be reckless and violent, Mitch's grades were decent, but his behavioral offenses were consistently off the charts.

This was that time when couples tended to be buttoned-down and conventional or *Ice Storm*-ish. Dana and Annie were neither—they were both. Completely devoted to each other, they were each other's only ever. They flirted and made eyes and messed around in the kitchen. If his mother's hands were full, Mitch says, you could be sure his father was groping her from behind. The children were left to be a little more independent than other kids, and it showed.

Then, one day in the midseventies, Dana went through a spiritual transformation. After listen-ing to a Christian self-help tape, he became demonstrative and interested in his children in a way he'd never been before. He reconciled with Mark and began studying: history, psychology, star formations. He became a scholar who was, in Mitch's words, "thirsty for information on every level." And he passed along to his younger son a fascination for all things—as well as a boundless sense of forgiveness and a near-deadly love for food.

Annie was a modern woman who worked outside the home—first as an RN, then as an interior designer—wore regal caftans, and threw legendary cocktail parties. She loved her kids with a dogged faith but perpetually questioned her own judgment. "I was never sure I was doing the whole mothering thing quite right," she says. But whether she did or she didn't, the family remains tight. Now eighty-one and the great-grandmother of four, her two remaining children (Mark died of cardiomyopathy in 1998) work and live within a couple miles of her downtown Minneapolis condominium. They see her daily and are devoted in a way unlike any other adult children I know.

Dana and Annie after fifty years

Dana died on the first day of May 2007, after fifty-eight years of marriage. For months Annie grieved fiercely, talking little, losing weight, hoping to go to sleep and never wake up. Mitch, Cynthia, and Libby took turns checking in—dragging Annie off to movies and camping out at her condo for what they called "slumber parties," though they were really interventions. In early 2008, Annie suddenly resurfaced. She was solemn and gentle but no longer living in darkness. And since that day, she and her son have sat around a table together at least four or five times a week.

Son and mother

As in the late sixties, when neighbors poured through the door every Friday night, Mitch and Annie eat together while surrounded by people, by laughter, by boisterous talk, and by thick, pungent cooking smells. For Annie Omer is today a fixture at the flagship Hell's Kitchen—tall and silver haired, in flowing black clothes—where Dana's caramel rolls and coleslaw and her own homemade mustard are served.

Annie's Mustard

½ cup dry mustard

½ cup sugar

½ cup flour

1 cup white vinegar

Mix dry mustard, sugar, and flour in a bowl. Heat vinegar to a boil, reduce heat to a simmer, and slowly stir in mustard mixture. Whisk continuously until thickened, about 1 minute. Remove from the heat, and let cool to room temperature, whisking occasionally. The mustard takes about 3 months to age and mellow properly. Will keep refrigerated damn near indefinitely. Makes 1¾ cups.

Cocktail Party Bean Dip

Mom got this recipe from her friend Adele, who was married to a guy named Tip who'd played football for the Chicago Bears in the thirties and forties. One day, I went over to their house, and there sat the ugliest man I'd ever seen, with a nose that covered half his face. Turned out it was the famous Bronko Nagurski, an All-American University of Minnesota and Hall of Fame Chicago Bears football player who played during the leather helmet days. That was a trip.

1 pound dried pinto beans

2 teaspoons kosher salt

2 tablespoons peanut oil

½ teaspoon dry mustard

1 large white onion, cut into chunks

1 cup (2 sticks) unsalted butter

½ pound provolone cheese, cubed

4 heaping teaspoons minced canned jalapeños

1 tablespoon liquid from canned jalapeños

¼ cup minced white onion

3 medium cloves garlic, mashed

Sort through dried beans, removing any debris such as small stones. Place in a large glass, stainless steel, or ceramic bowl, and cover with water. Soak 4 hours, drain and rinse.

Place soaked beans, salt, oil, mustard, and onion chunks in a large, heavy pot, and pour in 6 cups water, making sure beans are well covered. Heat to a boil. Reduce heat, cover, and simmer, checking occasionally, until beans are very soft, about 4 hours. If at any point evaporation exposes top layer of beans, add hot water to cover. Drain and return to the pot.

Mash beans with a potato masher. Stir together bean mixture, butter, provolone cheese, canned jalapeños, jalapeño liquid, minced onion, and mashed garlic.

Cook bean mixture over medium heat until cheese is absorbed, about 7 minutes. Serve hot with corn chips or saltine crackers. Makes approximately 8 cups.

Chile-Cheese Squares

6 eggs, beaten

1 cup all-purpose flour

1 cup whole milk

1 teaspoon baking powder

¼ teaspoon Jane's Krazy Mixed-Up Salt (or comparable seasoned salt)

4 cups (1 pound) shredded Monterey Jack cheese

1 (8-ounce) bag Mexican-style shredded cheese

2 ounces canned chopped green chiles

2 ounces canned chopped jalapeños

½ cup (1 stick) unsalted butter, melted

Preheat oven to 350°F.

Coat a 9 × 13–inch pan with a thin layer of butter to prevent sticking. Mix beaten eggs, flour, milk, baking powder, Jane's Krazy Mixed-Up Salt, Monterey Jack cheese, Mexican-style shredded cheese, and canned chiles and jalapeños in a large bowl. Stir in melted butter. Fold cheese mixture lightly into the pan with a rubber spatula.

Place on the center rack of the oven, and bake about 30 minutes, removing when cheese mixture bubbles and browns but is still soft. Cool before cutting, and reheat right before serving. These freeze very well in waxed paper. Makes about 35 squares.

Av. Head Cabbage - 2½ Lbs

Garlic Coleslaw.   10-12 Servings

1 Head Cabbage - Shredded   3½   For Best taste
2 Carrots - Chopped Fine   7   het set overNite
1 Bunch Green onions tops only - chopped Fine

     -Mix-
1 Qt Salad Dressing (Miracle whip)   Add Mix to Cabbage
7 oz Sugar - (1 heaping cup)   Start w/ ½ of Mix
½ oz Prepared Mustard (yellow) ⅓ cup   As Slaw varies +
Juice of ½ lemon   Bleeds
6 cloves garlic Mashed (½ Can of 4 oz Green Jalapenos)
Caynne Pepper to taste (½ tsp)

         (over)

For 50

4 heads Cabbage
10 Carrots - Chopped
½ c. Chopped Parsley   or 5 Bunches Green onion tops only
         Chopped Fine

1 Gal Salad Dressing (Miracle whip)
4 C.C Sugar   yellow
2½ oz Prepared Mustard (1 cup)
Juice 2½ Lemons
12 cloves garlic Mashed or 1, 4 oz Can Chopped Jalapenos
1 tsp Caynne Pepper

Curry Dip

1 cup Homemade Mayonnaise (see recipe, p. 147)

1 teaspoon tarragon vinegar

2 teaspoons grated white onion

1½ teaspoons prepared horseradish

1 teaspoon Homemade Hot Curry Powder (see recipe, p. 150)

¼ teaspoon garlic powder

Raw vegetables (baby carrots, cauliflower, broccoli, cherry tomatoes)

Mix mayonnaise, vinegar, onion, horseradish, curry powder, and garlic powder. Refrigerate for 3 hours to cool dip and meld flavors. Cut fresh vegetables just before serving. Makes 1¼ cups.

Garlic Coleslaw

Dad worked on his coleslaw for a long time. It had to have just the right amount of garlic and the right amount of cayenne. If you do it perfectly, it has the nicest kick. But this goddamn thing has been the bane of my existence in the restaurant. Every time I'd have my crew make it in large batches, they'd guess at the ratios of garlic and cayenne and get it wrong. Finally, I hung a sign above my salad prep area that read, "The coleslaw recipe is my dad's; follow the damn recipe." And I still have to occasionally ride their asses.

1 head green cabbage, cored and shredded

2 carrots, finely chopped

1 bunch (6 to 8) scallions, green parts only, sliced

1 quart Miracle Whip

1 heaping cup sugar

1 tablespoon prepared yellow mustard

½ lemon, juiced

6 medium cloves garlic, minced (2 tablespoons)

¼ cup canned chopped jalapeños

½ teaspoon cayenne

Mix cabbage, carrots, and scallions in a large bowl. In a separate bowl, mix Miracle Whip, sugar, mustard, lemon juice, garlic, jalapeños, and cayenne. Add Miracle Whip mixture slowly to vegetables, starting with half and using the rest as needed. Stop when cabbage is coated but not wet. For best taste, let sit in the refrigerator several hours or overnight. Makes 12 cups.

Dad

Great Napa Cabbage Salad

4 tablespoons (½ stick) unsalted butter

2 packages chicken-flavored ramen noodles, broken up

1 cup sugar, divided

¼ cup sesame seeds

1½ cups slivered almonds

⅓ cup apple cider vinegar

½ cup vegetable oil

¼ cup soy sauce

1 head napa cabbage, chopped

2 bunches (12 to 16) scallions, sliced

Melt butter over low heat in a heavy skillet. Add broken noodles, ½ cup of the sugar, sesame seeds, and almonds, and stir and cook until toasted and crunchy. Set aside and let cool. Whisk together remaining ½ cup sugar, apple cider vinegar, vegetable oil, and soy sauce. Place cabbage and scallions in a large bowl. Sprinkle cooled toasted-nut mixture over cabbage, and drizzle dressing over top. Makes 8 servings.

Aunt Frances

Aunt Fran's Chicken and Noodles

This dish is so fuckin' good it's unbelievable. Chicken gravy, pulled chicken, big, fat, homemade egg noodles, and mashed potatoes full of butter and cream. Mom was a nurse, and she worried that it was unhealthy. She was probably right, but she didn't dare say anything because she was afraid we'd just tell her Aunt Fran was a better cook and eat it anyway.

1 good-sized fatty fryer (3- to 4-pound whole chicken)

2 teaspoons kosher salt

4 quarts water

1½ pounds Egg Noodles (see recipe)

2 drops yellow food dye

2 to 3 tablespoons all-purpose flour

Dash ground black pepper

Dash cayenne

Dash celery salt

Dash garlic salt

Mitch's Mashed Potatoes (see recipe)

Prepare but do not cook Egg Noodles.

Wash and dry chicken thoroughly. Add salt to 4 quarts water, and boil chicken 1¼ hours. Remove chicken to a plate, and let cool.

Prepare Mitch's Mashed Potatoes, and cover to keep warm.

Chicken & Noodles

Boil washed & cleaned
whole chicken (I use a
good sized fatty fryer,
because their are tender)
Boil 1 hr - 15 min. Remove
chicken to plate to cool some.
Should have 3 - 3½ qts. broth (4 qts)
salt according to taste. I run
broth thru a colander to remove
small stuff. Set to pan & boil
(P.S. I add a couple drops of yellow food)
coloring to broth & to noodles, put a little
Drop noodles into broth & boil
slowly w/ lid on 25 min, stir occasionally
(over)

I leave quite a bit of flour on
my noodles, to make it thick
(add 3 T. flour mixed w/ water —

Noodles

4 eggs, beaten)
(2 tsp) ½ tsp salt
2 Tbs. water   Beat together
drop of yellow coloring   5 TBS CREAM — ½ CUP

Janis
pepper
sea salt
cayenne salt
celery salt
garlic salt

stir, shake + cut

Add flour ½ cu at a time
(maybe 2 cup?) until the dough
forms a firm lump. Place on heavily
floured board. let dry about 1 hr,
(roll thin) Cut into strips
let dry again, then stack & cut crosswise, car
be cooked at this point or freeze

Carve chicken, and pull meat from bones, leaving meat in chunks and shreds.

Run broth through a strainer, and reheat clear liquid to a boil. Drop in noodles. Cover and simmer 7 to 9 minutes, stirring occasionally (add food dye for color if desired). Remove from heat. If noodles were very floury, add 2 tablespoons of the flour to thicken broth into gravy; if gravy needs further thickening, add final tablespoon. Season noodles and broth with pepper, cayenne, celery salt, and garlic salt.

Mix noodles and broth with pulled chicken, and serve over hot mashed potatoes. Makes 8 servings.

EGG NOODLES

4 eggs

1½ teaspoons salt

3 tablespoons heavy cream

3 cups flour

Beat together eggs, salt, and milk or cream in a large bowl. Add ½ cup of the flour at a time to egg mixture and mix. Repeat until dough forms a firm lump. Place dough on a heavily floured board, and let dry about 1 hour.

Flour a rolling pin, and roll dough thin, keeping board and pin well floured to prevent sticking. Cut into strips with a sharp knife, and let dry 30 minutes. Noodles can be cooked at this point or frozen for later use. Makes 1½ pounds.

MITCH'S MASHED POTATOES

4 medium (about 3 pounds) russet potatoes, peeled and cut into 2-inch cubes

2 cups rich chicken broth

½ teaspoon kosher salt

4 tablespoons unsalted butter

½ cup heavy cream

Kosher salt

Ground black pepper

Simmer potatoes, chicken broth, and kosher salt in a saucepan over medium-high heat 17 to 21 minutes, or until tender. Drain stock, and reserve for making soups or sauces. Place potatoes in the bowl of a stand mixer, add butter, and beat on low speed. Add heavy cream, and mix until well incorporated. Season with salt and pepper. Makes 6 regular servings or 8 servings for chicken and noodles.

Frannie and Annie, dueling cooks

Special Occasion Goulash

This is my birthday meal . . . always
has been. Mom's original recipe
used hamburger, but growing up
with Graziano Brothers hot Italian
sausage, the best sausage in the
world, I made her change the recipe.
This is one of those rare foods that
I simply cannot fork into my mouth
fast enough.

1 pound Hot Italian Sausage
(see recipe, p. 134)

Or

1 pound bulk hot Italian sausage, or
remove casings from about 4 sausage
links

2 large yellow onions, chopped
(4 cups)

1 (15-ounce) can diced tomatoes,
with juice

2 teaspoons kosher salt

2 teaspoons cracked black pepper

1 cup ketchup

⅓ cup prepared yellow mustard

1 pound macaroni, cooked al dente
and drained

Heat a heavy skillet or Dutch oven over me-dium-high. Crumble sausage, and cook and stir until browned. Add onions, tomatoes, salt, pepper, ketchup, and mustard. Reduce heat to low, and simmer 20 minutes. Stir in macaroni, and cook for another 5 minutes before serving. Makes enough for 4 people . . . or half of a full serving for Mitch.

1960s-style Chicken Divan

The original recipe for this dish
came from *Better Homes & Gardens*,
but over the years and decades, mom
has continued to amend and refine
the recipe. Jesus, even now she
adjusts the ingredients and amounts
in an effort to make it better.
Personally, I think she's just
screwing with perfection.

4 (10-ounce) bags frozen broccoli

2 pounds boneless, skinless chicken
or turkey, roasted and cut into
pieces (see note)

2 (10½-ounce) cans condensed cream
of chicken soup

1 cup Homemade Mayonnaise
(see recipe, p. 147)

1 tablespoon lemon juice

1 teaspoon Homemade Hot Curry Powder
(see recipe, p. 150)

½ teaspoon cayenne, scant

2 cups shredded Cheddar cheese
(½ pound)

¾ cup bread crumbs

2 tablespoons unsalted butter,
melted

GOULASH (ANNIES)

1 # Lean Hamburger ⎫ Saute.
1 # Bulk Hot or Mild Sausage ⎬
1 or 2 Large Onions - Chopped. Rem meat - Saute
Onions in Drippings - Add meat After Onions
Cooked.
1 # Macaroni - Cooked Not Quite done
   Drain + Set Aside
Lg Can of tomatoes w/ Juice. Add to meat mix
   Pepperseeds - Salt + Pepper
1 C Catsup
1/3 C Yellow mustard
   Mix All Above - Cook Abt. 20 min
   Add Macaroni to mix. Heat Well.

Chicken Divan - BNG

350°

4 - frozen pkg. broccoli
2 # cooked chicken or turkey

2 cans cr. Chix soup ⎫
1 Ckup mayonnaise ⎪
1 T. lemon Jc (Jul lemon ⎬
1 t. curry pwd. ⎪
1/2 # Cheddar Cheese grated - ⎪
   cayenne 1/2 roan? ⎭
3/4 C. bread crumbs
1 - 2 T. butter -

arrange in
lg. bkg. dish
—
cover by
sauce -
grate cheese
all over top
crumbs over
all -
350° - 30 min

Preheat oven to 350°F.

Arrange broccoli and chicken or turkey pieces in a large, buttered baking dish. Mix soup, mayonnaise, lemon juice, curry powder, and cayenne in a bowl. Pour over meat and broccoli. Sprinkle shredded cheese over the top. Then sprinkle with bread crumbs, and drizzle with melted butter. Bake 30 minutes. Makes 8 servings.

NOTE: Mom uses a rotisserie chicken that can be purchased at nearly any deli or grocery store.

Ice Cream Puffs

Out by the airport on the south side of Des Moines was Johnny and Kay's. It was a nice little motel run by Johnny and Kay Campiano, and the restaurant and lounge were a throwback to the steak houses of the 1950s. But the treat for us kids was their ice cream puffs. Often the folks would pack us into the station wagon in our pajamas and go for a long ride in the summer evening, ending at Johnny and Kay's. The ice cream puffs were almost as big as our heads and remain today one of my favorite foods ever.

1 cup water

½ cup (1 stick) unsalted butter

1 tablespoon sugar

1 teaspoon kosher salt

1 cup all-purpose flour

3 to 4 large eggs

French vanilla ice cream

Fudge Sauce (see recipe)

Whipped Cream (see recipe)

Preheat oven to 425°F. Place a bowl and a whisk in the freezer for the whipped cream.

Heat water, butter, sugar, and salt in a heavy saucepan to a boil. Add flour and stir vigorously until dough forms and pulls away from the sides of the pan. Lower heat and continue stirring to dry out dough, about 3 minutes.

Remove the pan from heat, and scrape dough into the bowl of a stand mixer fitted with a

Libby ("the good one") with Mark and Mitch before proper diagnosis or federal warrants

paddle attachment. Turn mixer to low, and add eggs one at a time, mixing well after each addition. Before adding last egg, check consistency of dough. It should be thin enough to pipe but thick enough to hold a shape. If dough is too stiff, mix in last egg.

Remove dough from the mixer, and scrape into a pastry bag fitted with a star tip. Pipe 4 large balls onto a greased baking sheet, leaving at least 1 inch between each ball. Place on the center rack of the oven.

Bake 19 to 25 minutes, or until golden brown. Reduce heat to 200°F, and continue baking puffs to dry them out, another 21 to 27 minutes.

Remove puffs from the oven, let cool to room temperature, and then freeze. Once puffs are frozen, split each in half horizontally. Scoop ice cream into bottom halves of puffs, and top with other halves. Return ice cream puffs to the freezer.

Prepare Fudge Sauce and Whipped Cream.

To serve, warm fudge sauce in a saucepan over low heat. Drizzle fudge over frozen puffs, and top with whipped cream. Makes 4 servings.

FUDGE SAUCE

3 tablespoons unsalted butter

4 ounces dark chocolate

½ cup heavy cream

½ cup sugar

¾ cup cocoa powder

½ cup light corn syrup

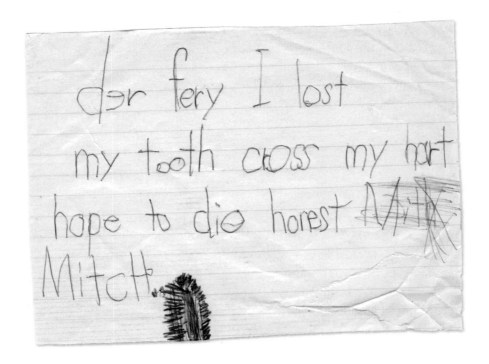

Fill a 2-quart saucepan with 3 cups of water, and bring to a simmer. Place all ingredients in a medium stainless steel, glass, or ceramic bowl, and place the bowl over the saucepan. Whisk continually until sugar dissolves and sauce smoothes and thickens, about 9 to 13 minutes. Cover and refrigerate. Sauce keeps for 3 weeks in the refrigerator and 3 months in the freezer. Makes 2 cups.

WHIPPED CREAM

1 cup heavy cream

¼ cup powdered sugar

1 teaspoon pure vanilla extract or Homemade Vanilla Extract (see recipe)

Prior to making whipped cream, place a bowl and a whisk in the freezer for at least 1 hour. Pour heavy cream into the bowl, and whisk vigorously or beat with a hand mixer until soft peaks form. Add powdered sugar and vanilla, and continue whisking or beating until firm peaks form. Cover and refrigerate. Makes 2 cups.

HOMEMADE VANILLA EXTRACT

1 vanilla bean

1 cup cognac

Split vanilla bean lengthwise, and scrape seeds into cognac. Chop pod into smaller pieces, and add to cognac. Store in an airtight container at room temperature for 1 month. Strain and return to the container. Will keep indefinitely. Makes 1 cup.

Dana's Caramel-Pecan Rolls

My dad hated small, hard caramel rolls, and he worked on this recipe for years until it was perfect. It's kind of an involved recipe, but he put a lot of time into it, so try not to fuck it up.

1¾ cups whole milk

⅓ cup honey

¼ cup vegetable shortening

1 package active dry yeast

1 extra-large egg

2 teaspoons kosher salt

4 to 5 cups all-purpose flour

1 cup granulated sugar

½ cup firmly packed dark brown sugar

2 tablespoons cinnamon

4 cups Caramel Sauce (see recipe)

½ cup (1 stick) unsalted butter, melted

3 cups Pecan Pieces (see recipe)

Preheat oven to 350°F.

Prepare Caramel Sauce and Pecan Pieces.

Heat milk, honey, and shortening in a saucepan until lukewarm, no more than 110°F. Remove from heat, and sprinkle yeast over milk mixture. After yeast blooms, about 5 minutes, pour mixture into the bowl of a stand mixture fitted with a dough hook or a paddle.

Add egg, salt, and 2 cups of the flour. Beat on medium speed for 5 to 7 minutes. Add remaining flour as needed until dough begins to pull away from the sides of the mixing bowl.

Take dough to a floured table, and knead until smooth and elastic. Cut dough in half. Roll each portion into a ball, and cover with a kitchen towel. Let rise until doubled in size, about 35 minutes. When risen, punch down and let rest for 11 more minutes.

Mix granulated sugar, brown sugar, and cinnamon.

Roll out each portion into a large rectangle ½ inch thick. Using half the melted butter, brush top of each portion, and sprinkle sugar mixture evenly. Roll into logs lengthwise, like a jelly roll. From logs, cut individual cinnamon rolls, 1½ to 1¾ inches thick.

Pour half of the caramel sauce into a 2 × 10 × 14–inch pan. Arrange rolls in the pan, cover with a kitchen towel, and allow to double in size. Remove the towel, and place the pan on the middle rack of the oven.

Bake 25 to 31 minutes, or until golden brown.

Remove the pan from the oven, and brush the rolls with remaining melted butter. Invert the pan onto a wire rack, separate rolls, and let cool.

To serve, ladle ¼ cup of the remaining warm caramel sauce over each roll, and sprinkle with pecan pieces. Makes 12 rolls.

CARAMEL SAUCE

Either

1 cup (2 sticks) unsalted butter

½ cup light corn syrup

3 cups firmly packed dark brown sugar

Or

3 cups firmly packed dark brown sugar

3 cups heavy cream

Place ingredients from either list in a saucepan, and slowly heat to a boil. Reduce heat, and simmer and stir until thick, about 9 minutes. Makes 4 cups.

PECAN PIECES

4 tablespoons (½ stick) unsalted butter

3 cups pecan pieces

2 teaspoons kosher salt

Melt butter in a skillet over medium-high heat. When butter begins to bubble, add pecan pieces and salt, stirring to mix well. Cook and stir pecans until browned, about 3 minutes. Remove from heat, and drain on a double thickness of paper towels. Makes 3 cups.

MAKING CARAMEL ROLLS

IN HELL

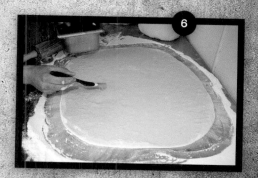

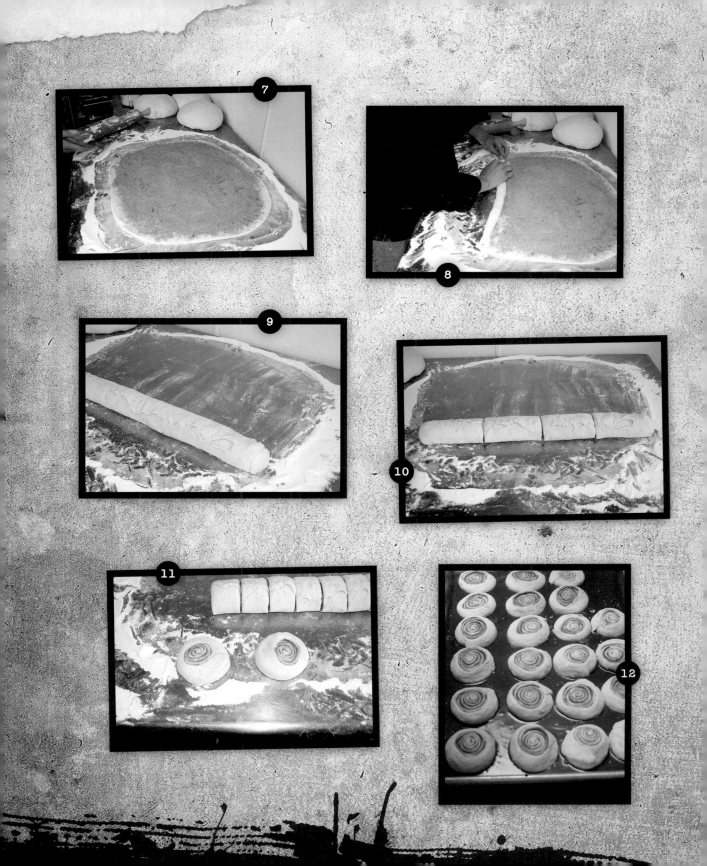

Hell's Kitchen
damn good food
Mitch Omer

DrUGS, SEX, And GLUttONy

Recipes from the Vagabond Years

Mental illness often intensifies when a young man reaches his late teens. But often, it goes unnoticed or is misidentified as hormones, laziness, or drug addiction. For Mitch it manifested as those things and much, much more.

He went to Iowa State on a football scholarship in 1973 (he was a varsity noseguard, bulky and mean) but walked off the field his freshman year. The university gave him another chance and took him back in 1974, but midseason he quit again. His parents were furious; they told him not to come home. So Mitch took off for Ely, Minnesota, where he'd worked at a resort a couple summers before, and spent a winter in the quiet northern Minnesota town—living off the grid in a remote cabin, shoveling driveways and doing odd jobs for money, and smoking a lot of grass.

He got to know an amateur pilot, who asked Mitch to fly cross-country to the man's home in Oklahoma. Mitch went along and promptly fell in love with the pilot's sixteen-year-old sister— Mitch was twenty-one—marrying her and moving with her to Minneapolis the next year.

"My family thought I was just an idiot," he says. "I had no money; I'd quit school; and I'd married a teenager," which essentially sums up Mitch's 1976.

Mitch took a job as a line cook at a deli, but that job came to an end when a broaster exploded and burned him, putting him out of work for several months. His next career move introduced him to two things, the rushes and highs you got from a real restaurant job— working as a manager at a hip, urban barbecue spot—and hard drugs. Mitch was an assistant manager. He greeted customers, seated people, and ran the servers, including his young wife. But his heart was in the kitchen with the cooks, who always had a supply of cocaine on hand.

He started snorting blow every night and then zipping through the dining room, making funny, charming small talk with the guests. When cocaine got too expensive, Mitch switched to crystal meth. And eventually, when even meth failed to send him, he started smoking PCP.

33

Perhaps the scariest thing was that he'd never been more energetic or functional. He did well at his job and learned the restaurant business like it was a second language. And thanks to the time he spent at the downtown rib joint hanging out in the kitchen, Mitch developed a feel for great barbecue.

Two decades later, in 1992, his original recipe took the blue ribbon at the Star Tribune National Rib Cook-off.

Mitch's Barbecue Ribs

These are wet ribs, as opposed to dry, where no sauce is added. In the business, brushing the sauce on is called "mopping."

4 racks (6 to 7 pounds) baby back ribs

½ cup Rose's lime juice

5 tablespoons hot paprika

4 tablespoons granulated garlic

4 tablespoons ground cumin

4 tablespoons dark chili powder

4 tablespoons granulated sugar

4 tablespoons dark brown sugar

4 tablespoons ground black pepper

3 tablespoons kosher salt

2 tablespoons cayenne

Barbecue Sauce (see recipe)

Brush ribs with Rose's lime juice. Mix paprika, garlic, cumin, chili powder, sugar, brown sugar, black pepper, salt, and cayenne in a large bowl. Sprinkle rib rub liberally over ribs. Refrigerate for at least 4 hours, or overnight. Store leftover rib rub in an air-tight container.

Preheat oven to 200°F.

Remove ribs from the refrigerator, and bring to room temperature. Place ribs on a rimmed baking sheet, and put on the middle rack of the oven. Bake 3 hours.

At this point, ribs can be refrigerated for later use, up to 3 days.

Make Barbecue Sauce.

Start a charcoal or wood fire in a grill, allowing coals to burn down and spread out so the heat is even. Place ribs on the grill and cook, depending on the heat, 11 to 17 minutes per side. You want the ribs to develop a crust on the outside and be heated through. Brush both sides of ribs with barbecue sauce, and grill each side again until sauce has caramelized a bit.

Remove ribs from the grill, and slice between each bone. Serve with a side of my dad's coleslaw (recipe, p. 15). Makes 4 to 8 servings.

BARBECUE SAUCE

2 cups Open Pit barbecue sauce

1 small white onion, chopped (½ cup)

4 tablespoons dark brown sugar

3 tablespoons honey

2 tablespoons red wine vinegar

2 tablespoons crushed red pepper

2 tablespoons dark molasses

2 tablespoons Worcestershire sauce

2 teaspoons liquid smoke

Place Open Pit in a large saucepan, and warm over medium-high heat. Purée onion in a food processor fitted with a steel chopping blade, and scrape into the saucepan. Stir in remaining ingredients. Heat mixture to a boil over high, stirring continually. Reduce heat and simmer 19 to 21 minutes, stirring occasionally. Let sauce cool to room temperature and refrigerate. Makes 3½ cups.

Mitch's first marriage came to an end when he discovered his wife was having an affair with a busboy. Shortly after, his job did, too.

"I wanted to kill the guy, and I still worked with him, which was a problem," Mitch says. "So I moved on."

He took his homicidal attitude to a Minneapolis biker bar called the Cabooze, where he worked as a bouncer. There were live bands every night and plenty of beautiful women in halter tops and tight jeans. Even better, he was getting paid to be an asshole. But after a year of shoving guys around, Mitch started to get really mean. His mood would change in a flash—one minute he'd be watching the door, the next

he'd be pounding on some guy who'd grabbed some girl's ass. His roommate at the time tried to help Mitch by turning him on to LSD.

It worked. Suddenly, everything got better. The music sounded good again, and Mitch was happier (score one point, at least, for self-medication). He kept himself in check by tripping for years.

It was at the Cabooze that Mitch met his second wife, Jill. He also got a job cooking at a natural foods restaurant chain called the Good Earth, and in 1979 the two moved to Colorado. Mitch was still cooking. Then Jill got pregnant, and in order to make more money, he hired on with a security company to work as a guard for touring rock bands.

It was the perfect life for someone who loved drugs and music. Back home, Jill had given birth to their son, Casey. Mitch loved the baby. He also loved being on the road. Over the next couple years, he toured with the Rolling Stones, Carlos Santana, the Temptations, Frank Zappa, and the Allman Brothers.

Most of the musicians Mitch met were great. But Van Halen disgusted him. Not only were they rude to the roadies, the band members made ridiculous demands. For instance, at each concert stop they ordered five pounds of M&M's *with all the brown ones removed.* Production coordinators spent hours poring through bags of M&M's, Mitch says, picking out the brown ones. But someone at an arena in Colorado Springs refused and brought the band a bowl that included brown M&M's. Van Halen responded by trashing the place, including smearing lasagna into the stage drapery.

Lasagna, Van Halen Style

Rock bands are known for their eccentricities and excesses. The Who threw televisions out the windows of their hotel rooms; Led Zeppelin raced motorcycles up and down the halls. But Van Halen protests the inclusion of brown M&M's by smearing lasagna in the drapery at the arena? Outrageous!

2 eggs, beaten

1 (16-ounce) container whole milk ricotta cheese

⅓ cup (1 ounce) grated Parmesan cheese

8 cups Tomato-Red Pepper Sauce with Hot Italian Sausage (see recipe), divided

9 Homemade Lasagna Noodles (see recipe), divided

3 cups (12 ounces) shredded low-moisture mozzarella cheese, divided

Prepare Tomato–Red Pepper Sauce with Hot Italian Sausage, and Homemade Lasagna Noodles.

Preheat oven to 375°F.

Combine eggs, ricotta, and Parmesan in a bowl.

Spread ½ cup of the sauce, just enough for a thin coating, over the bottom of an enameled cast iron or stainless steel 13 × 9–inch baking pan.

Arrange 3 of the noodles lengthwise in a slightly overlapping layer over sauce, and trim ends to fit the pan. Spread evenly half of the cheese mixture over noodles, and sprinkle evenly 1 cup of the shredded mozzarella over cheese mixture. Spoon evenly half of the remaining sauce over mozzarella.

Arrange 3 more of the noodles over sauce, and trim ends. Spread remaining half of the cheese mixture over noodles, and sprinkle 1 cup of the shredded mozzarella over cheese mixture. Spoon remaining half of the sauce over mozzarella.

Arrange last 3 noodles over sauce, and trim ends. Sprinkle remaining 1 cup shredded mozzarella over noodles.

Place baking pan on a rimmed baking sheet, and bake 40 to 45 minutes, or until golden brown. Let cool 10 minutes before serving.

To serve, spread lasagna evenly over carpet and drapes, and sit down to a bowl of M&M's (brown ones optional).

TOMATO-RED PEPPER SAUCE WITH HOT ITALIAN SAUSAGE

3 large roasted red peppers (see method in Roasted Red Pepper Purée, p. 155)

1 pound Hot Italian Sausage (see recipe, p. 134)

Or

1 pound bulk hot Italian sausage or 4 sausage links with the casings removed

1 large white onion, finely chopped (2 cups)

3 medium cloves garlic, minced
(1 tablespoon)

1½ pounds vine-ripened tomatoes,
coarsely chopped

2 teaspoons dried thyme

2 teaspoons dried basil

2 teaspoons fennel seeds

1 teaspoon crushed red pepper

½ teaspoon ground black pepper

Prepare Hot Italian Sausage.

Purée roasted red peppers in a food processor fitted with a steel chopping blade.

Add sausage to a 2-quart saucepan, and cook over medium-high heat until meat is brown. Remove sausage with a slotted spoon and reserve. Heat rendered sausage fat in the saucepan over medium high, and cook onions and garlic, stirring constantly, for 1 minute. Stir in puréed red peppers, tomatoes, thyme, basil, fennel, crushed red pepper, and black pepper. Crumble the cooked sausage, and add to sauce.

Heat sauce to a boil, and then reduce heat. Cover and simmer for 15 minutes, stirring occasionally. Makes 8 cups.

HOMEMADE LASAGNA NOODLES

2½ cups all-purpose flour

4 large, fresh basil leaves, finely chopped

2 teaspoons crushed red pepper

3 tablespoons + 1 teaspoon kosher salt, divided

2 large eggs

8 quarts + ⅓ cup water, divided

5 tablespoons + 2 teaspoons extra-virgin olive oil, divided

Add flour, basil, crushed red pepper, 1 teaspoon of the kosher salt, and eggs to a food processor fitted with a steel chopping blade. Cover and pulse until mixture resembles coarse meal.

While running the food processor, slowly add ⅓ cup of the water and 2 teaspoons of the olive oil through the feed tube. Continue running the food processor until dough forms a ball, gradually adding additional flour as necessary until dough pulls cleanly away from the sides.

Transfer dough to a lightly floured surface. Cover with a kitchen towel, and let rest 10 minutes. Divide dough into 4 equal portions. Roll each portion with a lightly floured rolling pin into a rough, large rectangle, and trim down to 14 × 10–inch rectangles. Let rest 30 minutes.

Cut dough rectangles lengthwise into thirds to form noodles.

Heat to a boil 8 quarts of the water in a 12-quart pot. Add 3 tablespoons of the kosher salt and 4 tablespoons of the olive oil. Add 6 of the noodles, and cook about 2 minutes.

Drain noodles in a colander, and cook remaining 6 noodles. Toss noodles lightly with remaining 1 tablespoon of olive oil in a large bowl. Makes 12 noodles.

Mitch quit working security for rock bands after the Waylon Jennings tour of 1981. Buff from all the equipment hauling he'd been doing—about 300 pounds of solid muscle—and strung out on drugs, he caught a kid trying to steal from the band, got him down on the ground, and started kicking him but couldn't stop. The kid nearly died. Mitch realized he had to return home and get control of himself.

He and Jill had a good year, during which their daughter, Jesse, was born. Mitch was

Mitch and Casey during the good years

cooking again, at a steakhouse called Bananas, and really enjoying himself in the kitchen for the first time. They moved back to the Twin Cities in the early 1980s when he got an offer to work as a baker for a high-end hotel. He quickly developed baker's asthma (for which he uses an inhaler to this day), but Mitch had fallen in love with the culinary arts, so much so that he went to the best restaurant he could think of—the New French Café—and offered to cook for three months with no pay if they would take him on.

It worked. And with a job in what was then the most prestigious kitchen in town, Mitch was on fire. He hung out with Alexander Dixon, the executive chef, after hours and soaked up every bit of wisdom he could. He started writing his own recipes, keeping a cookbook of his own. This was his apprenticeship, and by the time Mitch moved on from New French, he'd become—in every sense—a real chef.

Recipes from the New French Café

The New French Café was an incredible proving ground for any good cook or aspiring chef. No matter how exotic the ingredient, you had only to ask, and it would show up at the restaurant the next day. These recipes are very involved, far more than what I'm making in the restaurant today. But that's how New French was. We experimented with absolutely everything!

Jalapeño-Polenta Blinis with Sour Cream, Chives, and Caviar

½ cup whole milk

1 large egg

1 tablespoon unsalted butter, melted

2 or 3 fresh jalapeños, seeded and minced (3 tablespoons)

¼ cup all-purpose flour

¼ cup polenta (coarse-ground yellow cornmeal)

1 teaspoon baking powder

¼ teaspoon kosher salt

¼ teaspoon ground cumin

3 tablespoons unsalted butter

36 (1-inch) lengths cut chives

¼ cup sour cream

1 ounce good caviar or salmon roe

Whisk together milk, egg, melted butter, and jalapeños in a medium bowl. Mix flour, polenta, baking powder, salt, and cumin in another bowl. Slowly add polenta mixture to egg mixture, continuously stirring vigorously. Refrigerate batter for at least 1 hour.

Melt 3 tablespoons butter in a large nonstick skillet over medium-high heat. Drop batter in hot butter in 2-tablespoon portions, making 12 blinis. You may need to fry these in two batches.

Flip blinis when bottoms begin to brown and small bubbles push through batter, about 2 to 5 minutes. Cook 1 more minute. Remove blinis from the skillet, and drain on a double thickness of paper towels.

To serve, arrange 3 of the chive lengths on each blini, fanning out from the center. Place a 1-teaspoon dollop of the sour cream in the center, on top of chives. Divide caviar between each blini. Makes 4 servings.

Lobster Risotto with Roe and Fresh Peas

4½ cups Lobster Broth (see recipe)

4 ounces (about 1 cup) shelled fresh peas

4 tablespoons (½ stick) unsalted butter

2 medium shallots, thinly sliced (½ cup)

1½ cups Arborio rice

Tail meat from Lobster, coarsely chopped (see recipe)

Roe from Lobster (see recipe)

⅓ cup grated Parmesan cheese (1 ounce)

2 tablespoons freshly grated lemon zest

2 tablespoons fresh lemon juice

2 tablespoons finely chopped fresh parsley

2 tablespoons minced fresh chives

Kosher salt

Ground black pepper

8 lobster claws

Prepare Lobster and Lobster Broth.

Place lobster broth in a saucepan, and heat to a boil. Reduce heat and add peas. Simmer 2 to 3 minutes, just until bright green. Strain peas from broth, and run peas under cold water to stop cooking. Set aside. Allow stock to continue simmering.

Melt butter in a large, heavy saucepan over medium-high heat. Add shallots and cook and stir until translucent, about 3 minutes. Add rice and stir vigorously, coating evenly in shallots and butter.

Add ½ cup of the lobster broth, and stir with a wooden spoon until absorbed, about 1 to 2 minutes. Add another ½ cup of the broth, and stir until absorbed. Continue adding broth in ½-cup increments, stirring until absorbed. The whole process should take about 15 to 21 minutes, and the rice should be creamy but firm and not mushy. You may not need the last ½ cup of the broth.

Remove from heat, and stir in lobster tail meat, lobster roe, and cooked peas. Stir in Parmesan, lemon zest, lemon juice, parsley, and chives, mixing well. Season with salt and pepper.

Divide risotto among 4 plates, and top each plate with 2 lobster claws. Makes 4 servings.

LOBSTER

1 gallon water

¼ cup kosher salt

4 (1¼-pound) live female lobsters (see note)

Pour water and salt into a large stock pot, and heat to a boil.

Using a large chef's knife, make a deep slit in each lobster's head to kill it. Make an incision where the soft fin-like appendages meet the tails on the underside of lobsters. Remove roe and reserve.

Immerse lobsters head first into boiling water, let water return to a boil, and simmer 5 minutes. Remove the pot from the heat, and drain water. Remove lobsters from the pot, and run cold water over them to stop cooking. Let lobsters cool.

Remove meat from tails and reserve. Crack claws and delicately remove meat whole and reserve. Reserve lobster shells.

NOTE: Female lobsters are sweeter than their male counterparts and hold the roe needed for this recipe.

LOBSTER BROTH

Shells from Lobster, coarsely chopped

⅓ cup unsalted butter

⅓ cup dry white wine

6 cups rich chicken broth

Add chopped lobster shells and butter to a large pot. Cook over medium-high heat, stirring continually, for 11 minutes. Add wine and chicken broth, and heat to a boil. Reduce heat and simmer, uncovered, until total liquid, minus shells, reduces to 4½ cups. Strain through a fine mesh sieve, and discard solids. Makes 4½ cups.

Charred Tuna with Beurre Noisette

2 tablespoons hot paprika

1 tablespoon sea salt

1 teaspoon ground black pepper

1 teaspoon ground white pepper

1 teaspoon onion powder

1 teaspoon garlic powder

¾ teaspoon dried thyme

¾ teaspoon dried oregano

¾ teaspoon cayenne

4 (6- to 7-ounce) sushi-grade ahi tuna fillets

4 tablespoons (½ stick) unsalted butter, melted

4 tablespoons (½ stick) + ⅓ cup unsalted butter

½ fresh lemon

Mix paprika, salt, black pepper, white pepper, onion powder, garlic powder, thyme, oregano, and cayenne in a small bowl.

Brush one side of each tuna fillet with melted butter, and generously season with paprika mixture, pressing seasoning into the flesh. Cover and refrigerate at least 2 hours.

Take fillets out of the refrigerator, and bring to room temperature.

Heat 4 tablespoons of the unmelted butter in a large, heavy skillet over high, until it just begins to smoke. Add fillets, seasoned side down, and sear until they appear burnt, about 2 minutes. Turn fillets over, and cook another 30 seconds.

Remove fillets from the skillet, and place on serving plates.

Discard butter from the skillet, but don't wipe it clean. Return the skillet to the heat. Add remaining ⅓ cup butter, and melt over high heat until it just begins to smoke. Squeeze lemon over butter, and remove the skillet from the heat.

Drizzle burnt butter over fillets and serve. Makes 4 servings.

Crispy Salmon with Caramelized Shallots, Lemon, and Bacon

4 (6- to 7-ounce) wild Coho salmon fillets

4 tablespoons (½ stick) unsalted butter, melted

4 tablespoons lemon pepper

¾ cup panko bread crumbs (see note)

½ cup polenta (coarse-ground yellow cornmeal)

¼ cup peanut oil

2 pieces of thick-sliced bacon, finely chopped

8 large shallots, thickly sliced (about 1 cup)

Zest from ½ lemon

2 tablespoons balsamic vinegar

2 teaspoons fresh lemon juice

3 tablespoons cold unsalted butter, cut into small pieces

2 teaspoons kosher salt

2 teaspoons ground black pepper

Preheat oven to 375°F.

Brush top and bottom of fillets with melted butter, using all of the butter. Season top and bottom of each fillet with lemon pepper. Mix bread crumbs and polenta in a small bowl. Divide bread crumb mixture among 4 fillets, and press into top and bottom of fillets firmly. Let rest 31 minutes.

Heat peanut oil in a large, heavy skillet over medium high until hot but not smoking. Add fillets, skin side up. Cook until brown crust forms, about 1½ minutes. Turn fillets over, and cook another 15 seconds. Remove the skillet from the heat, and place in the oven for 2 to 5 minutes. Remove the skillet from the oven, and plate the fillets.

Place chopped bacon in a different large skillet, and cook over medium-high heat. Cook and stir until bacon is crisp and all bacon fat has been rendered. Spoon bacon pieces out of the skillet with a slotted spoon and reserve. Add shallots, and cook in rendered bacon fat until they begin to brown, about 7 to 9 minutes. Add lemon zest, balsamic vinegar, and lemon juice.

Cook and stir until sauce begins to thicken, about 5 minutes. Remove the skillet from the heat, and stir in 3 tablespoons cold butter vigorously. Add crisp bacon pieces, and season with salt and pepper. Spoon sauce over fillets, and serve immediately. Makes 4 servings.

NOTE: You can get these Japanese–style bread crumbs at most grocery stores, or you can substitute dry bread crumbs. But NEVER use stale bread—that only makes for stale bread crumbs.

Mitch left the New French Café—reluctantly—in 1984 when he was offered an executive chef position at a historic restaurant in Minneapolis's riverfront district called Pracna on Main. And there he met Steve Meyer, the sous chef who would become his first lieutenant for life.

Mitch and Steve: kindred spirits, partners in crime

They were a striking pair—Mitch, six foot five in his cowboy boots, and Steve, a small, dark man who looked like he stepped out of a Mario Bros. game and was legally required to use a special booster seat when he drove. Where Mitch was wild and creative, always searching for exotic ingredients and combinations no one else had thought of, Steve was a no-nonsense workaday cook. He could stand on his feet behind the hot line for eight, ten, twelve hours and turn out a menu item every couple of minutes. He was like a machine.

There was very little experimental edge to his cooking—that was Mitch's department—but Steve was the perfect foil to a head chef with cloud-level highs and devastating lows. As consistent as sunrise, Steve showed up at the same time each day and kept the kitchen running. More than twenty-five years later, he still does.

The one thing the two men shared was an ability to drink the entire beer list . . . then move on to kamikazes. In fact, Steve—who easily weighed half of what Mitch once did—often drank his superior under the table and then stepped over him and continued on.

Nevertheless, at Pracna, Mitch continued working in the culinary fever he'd caught at New French.

Mitch and Steve's Oversize Kamikazes

Your standard kamikaze is one ounce each lime juice, triple sec, and vodka. Sweet, but it takes all of two seconds to drink. So we rounded the recipe up to an exact pint. We usually ended up barking like raccoons by the end of the night.

5 ounces Rose's lime juice

5 ounces Cointreau

6 ounces Stolichnaya vodka

Lime wedge

Mix ingredients in a large cocktail shaker over ice and shake vigorously. Pour into a large glass, garnish with a lime wedge, and drink. Makes 1 serving. Triple recipe for a pitcher.

Recipes from Pracna

Pracna was a great place to develop my own menu, and style. After about a year there, however, the owners enlisted a new general manager who proceeded to completely usurp my menu and staffing. All foods were to be brought in preprocessed, and my higher-salaried cooks were to be dismissed in favor of minimum-wage prep cooks. To roll this new direction out, they wanted me to address the staff. In my starched white chef's coat, with Steve by my side and the new GM looking on, I said I could simply not endorse this new menu and staff cuts and walked out.

Salmon Tartare with Buttered Brioche Toast Points

3 slices Brioche Bread (see recipe, p. 203)

⅓ cup unsalted butter, melted

1 pound sushi-grade salmon, finely chopped

1 small clove garlic, minced (½ teaspoon)

3 tablespoons capers, drained and minced

⅓ cup minced red onion

4 tablespoons minced fresh chives

3 tablespoons toasted sesame seeds

1 tablespoon extra-virgin olive oil

1 tablespoon sesame oil

1 tablespoon fresh lemon juice

2 teaspoons freshly grated lemon zest

2 teaspoons wasabi paste

Sea salt

Ground black pepper

3 tablespoons Annie's Mustard (see recipe, p. 12)

4 tablespoons salmon roe

Preheat oven to 375°F.

Cut crusts from brioche bread, leaving 3 squares. Brush both sides of bread with melted butter. Cut each square diagonally twice, creating 4 triangles per slice. Place bread on a rimmed baking sheet, and place on the middle rack of the oven. Bake until just toasted but not crisp, about 7 to 9 minutes. Remove from the oven, and let cool to room temperature.

Mince together chopped salmon, minced garlic, and chopped capers with a large chef's knife. Place salmon mixture in a large bowl, and fold in red onion, chives, sesame seeds, olive oil, sesame oil, lemon juice, lemon zest, and wasabi paste. Season with salt and pepper.

Mound tartare in the center of each plate. Drizzle each mound with mustard, and sprinkle salmon roe on top. Arrange 3 toast points on each plate and serve. Makes 4 servings.

Poached Halibut with Peas and Crawfish

12 whole crawfish, boiled

7 tablespoons unsalted butter, divided

2 cups Fish Fumet (see recipe)

1½ cups shelled fresh peas

⅓ cup crushed wasabi peas

4 (6- to 7-ounce) halibut fillets

Fresh pea tendrils

Sea salt

Ground black pepper

Remove tail meat from crawfish and set aside. Crush crawfish shells with a mortar and pestle.

Melt 4 tablespoons of the butter in a large skillet over medium-high heat. Add crawfish shells to the skillet, and cook and stir for 5 to 7 minutes. Add fish fumet, and simmer uncovered another 5 to 7 minutes. Remove the skillet from the heat, and strain broth through a double thickness of cheesecloth into a saucepan. Wipe the skillet, and discard solids.

Place 1 cup of the broth in the skillet, and heat to a boil. Add fresh peas, and heat just through, about 1 minute. Skim peas from broth with a slotted spoon, reserving 20 whole peas for garnish. Place remaining peas in a food processor fitted with a steel chopping blade. Process peas until coarsely chopped, about 5 seconds. Add remaining 3 tablespoons butter, and process peas another 5 to 7 seconds. Set aside pea purée.

Add halibut fillets to the skillet, and heat until broth boils. Reduce heat, cover, and simmer. Poach fillets 5 to 7 minutes. Remove the skillet from the heat.

Heat remaining crawfish broth in the saucepan to a boil.

Divide pea purée, and spoon onto the center of 4 plates. Top pea purée with poached fillets. Spoon crawfish broth onto plates, and garnish each plate with 5 whole peas and 3 crawfish tails. Sprinkle crushed wasabi peas over each fillet. Season with salt and pepper, and garnish plates with pea tendrils. Makes 4 servings.

FISH FUMET

2 tablespoons unsalted butter

1 medium celery rib, finely chopped

1 small carrot, peeled and finely chopped

1 small onion, peeled and finely chopped

1 small clove garlic, finely chopped

2 pounds flatfish bones (sole or halibut), coarsely chopped

1 cup dry white wine

8 cups cold water

3 whole black peppercorns

4 parsley stems, finely chopped

½ bay leaf

1 whole clove

Pinch dried thyme

Heat butter in a heavy-bottomed stock pot or a large saucepan over medium-high. Add celery, carrot, onion, and garlic, and sweat vegetables about 5 minutes, or until onions are translucent. Do not brown the vegetables.

Add fish bones, and sweat about 3 minutes, until bones are opaque. Add wine, and bring to a boil. Add water, peppercorns, parsley, bay leaf, clove, and thyme, and return to a boil. Reduce heat immediately, and simmer uncovered 31 to 45 minutes.

Strain fumet through a fine mesh strainer and again through a double thickness of cheesecloth. Let cool to room temperature, cover, and refrigerate. Makes 8 cups

From Pracna, Mitch took a job that he thought would be his biggest break yet. It turned out to be the beginning of his undoing. As executive chef of the Atrium—a multistory restaurant and banquet hall in a newly gentrified area of the city—he fell flat on his ass.

"The scale of what we were doing—a seven-course sit-down dinner for 1,700—it was just out of my league." Mitch tells this story with wide, honest eyes. "Fuck, I made a mess of it. I was just falling down all the time."

The final humiliation came on the night he was fired. Mitch had brought Dana in that night because British royalty were coming through the Atrium and his dad had always wanted to attend a real high tea. While father was drinking Earl Grey, son was given his pink slip and ushered out the door.

Mitch was thirty-three at this point, and he believed he'd already peaked in the food business. So he moved his family, which now included three children (Lauren was born in 1985), to California, where he apprenticed as a beer brewer. But shortly after arriving there, he discovered his wife had been having an affair with his best friend for the past five years (while Mitch was working late, they'd been making like dolphins in his own bed).

He divorced, lost his daughters (who went with their mother), and picked up a series of women, including one he talked into having sex in the mash tun at Devil Mountain Brewery. Professional brewers are regulated by the Bureau of Alcohol, Tobacco, and Firearms—

a pretty humorless lot. When word spread (as it inevitably did), they could easily have shut the brewery down. Instead, Mitch was simply fired, again. He went to work at Buffalo Bill's where he ended up in bed with the owner's girlfriend. Again, he lost his job.

He moved back to Minnesota and went to work with his old friend Steve Meyer at a restaurant called the Pickled Parrot. But both men were drinking heavily, and they had a falling out. When management came in to settle things, they decided Mitch had been in the wrong. And this time when he was fired, it stuck.

Drug addled and heavier than he'd ever been, Mitch took his son and moved back to Ely for the third time in his life. There, he sank into a serious depression, and the only thing that helped was eating. Before the winter of 1995 was over, he weighed 420 pounds. He was so fat that even living in northern Minnesota, where temperatures often dropped to twenty and thirty degrees below zero, he was impervious to the cold. Sometimes, he would take a sauna and then thunder through the woods naked, long white hair flying behind him. After one occasion, the newspaper ran a story about a skier who spotted a Yeti. Everyone in town knew it was Mitch.

Twice, he seriously contemplated suicide. The only thing stopping him was his teenage son in the bedroom next door. His comforts were simple. Days, he hung out at

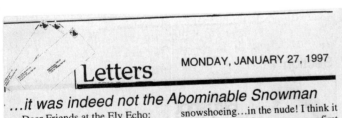

Letters

MONDAY, JANUARY 27, 1997

...it was indeed not the Abominable Snowman

Dear Friends at the Ely Echo:

Yeti lives! Yesterday evening (January 22), just before sunset, a group of us, five in all, were cross-country skiing the trails below Passi Hill, when we noticed a large, white beast moving through the snow on a ridge above us.

I know this sounds farfetched, but as God is my witness, I am telling the truth. It was a large animal, almost 6-1/2 feet tall by our collective reasoning, and with long white hair.

The hair, however, was only on the head. As we paused breathlessly to study its habits, we soon learned that it was indeed not the Abominable Snowman, but a rather large man

snowshoeing…in the nude! I think it was the tattoos that gave us our first clue as to the true nature of the beast.

I realize that residents of these northern climes pride themselves on their hardy stock; but this man was, or seemed, perfectly content to plow through the woods, in the middle of a snowstorm, buck nekkid!

It was a wonder we shall not soon forget, and seemed a fitting finale to an incredible week of winter camping in the Boundary Waters Canoe Area Wilderness.

Sincerely,
Jim Davidson
San Francisco, CA

Four hundred pounds of joy and depression

Once his moods were on an even keel, Mitch realized there was no way he could fight the monster his body had become. At 420 pounds he could barely walk, much less exercise. And his stomach was so stretched out it was impossible to know how much to eat. He found a doctor who was willing to perform gastric bypass surgery, and like magic the weight began to fall off. After a hundred pounds or so, he was confident enough to begin applying for jobs.

And at the age of forty-five, Mitch Omer got his life back—ironically, with the help of drugs.

a local bicycle shop with Pappy, who would become his closest friend. Nights, he worked as a radio DJ, making just enough to visit Kentucky Fried Chicken six or seven times a week and buy a lot of cheap beer.

By the age of forty-three, Mitch believed he was a hopeless case. Broke, obese, strung out, and stranded up north, he was mostly cut off from his family, was a miserable father, and hadn't had actual sex (anonymous phone sex, he says, is another story) in more than five years.

Then, he walked into a psychiatrist's office and told his story, and the man diagnosed manic depression (now called bipolar disorder) and obsessive-compulsive traits, prescribing an antidepressant that was only marginally helpful. But this tiny bit of progress—and clarity—galvanized Mitch to seek better treatment in the Cities. There, he found a doctor who gave him a cocktail of meds, including new-fangled antipsychotics recently approved for bipolar and OCD.

Mitch, starting over at forty-five

MANIC CUISINE

By 2000, Mitch had lost nearly half his body weight and had stabilized at around 245 pounds. He'd quit eating, drinking, and drugging himself to death. His moods had leveled out. And he'd been working the same job—as chef at a quaint riverside inn just outside of St. Paul—for over a year. That's when Annie convinced him it was time to date again. And she helped him post a personal ad on AOL's singles site.

The following day, a woman named Cynthia Gerdes responded:

If you have a wonderful and witty sense of humor, if you're honest beyond reproach (be truthful or you'll toss 'n turn all night), if you understand integrity, if you're fun, if you are sane and insane at the same (sane?) time, if you like what you do for a living (or are taking steps in that direction), if you love Seinfeld, if you're a wonderful dad, if you are financially stable, if you aren't pulling a SmartCart piled high with baggage, AND (here we go . . . this is where most guys trip up) if you really can SHARE emotions (up OR down), if you are introspective, if you know how to communicate, if you aren't afraid to cry, and if you LIKE your life but are truly looking for a well-adjusted, happy soulmate, read on . . .

Her response went on for another nine paragraphs in exactly the same 90-miles-per-hour fashion, and Mitch was entranced. He wrote back. Then, curious, he showed up at the toy store where she'd told him she worked. It wasn't until he asked for her by name that he found out she owned the store, plus six more.

Technically, Cynthia was still married at the time. She and her husband of more than twenty years had decided to divorce only a couple days before she spied Mitch's personal ad, yet on a calculated whim—which is her modus operandi, a symptom, she claims, of deeply entrenched ADHD—Cyn answered it, figuring she might as well get started because it would take hundreds of attempts to find the man of her dreams.

Not so. Mitch and Cyn fell in love at their

first meeting and charged ahead, planning a March 2001 wedding, complicating their own lives and the lives of everyone around them. She had to rush her divorce in order to remarry . . . and explain to Katy, her teenage daughter, who was suspicious that her mother had broken up her marriage by having an affair. Even while the family roiled, Mitch moved into Cynthia's staid, suburban home with his voluminous collections: electric guitars, books, records, and guns. His newfound stability teetered, but he was happier than he'd ever been in his life.

Mitch and Cyn on their wedding day

For a year or so, they partied and traveled and worked at their respective jobs, enjoying a life together that neither had imagined possible. Then the little inn where Mitch was working happily as executive chef was sold, and the new owners fired the entire staff. Discouraged and spiraling down, Mitch complained that he was tired of making money for other people.

Cyn, full of insomniac energy and willfully confident in her brand-new husband, gave him a shove.

"Start your own place," she said. "I'll help for a while."

They conspired to open a restaurant that would combine her business sense with Mitch's cooking and his various obsessions—rich, buttery food; alcohol; rock 'n' roll—as well as his extensive collection of Gothic art. A family member told them about a dank, crooked little building on the edge of downtown Minneapolis, between a wig shop and an appliance store, that they could actually afford. They sold everything they had, including Cynthia's home and both their cars, and borrowed the rest of their start-up capital from Annie and Dana, who believed in the concept from the start. From the very beginning, Cyn handled the financial end of things and Mitch developed the menus. He asked Steve, his perennial sous chef, to join as a minority third partner and manage the kitchen. Steve's wife, Kim, signed up to run the front of the house.

Together, the two couples painted the walls crimson, scoured the earth for black linens (this was before other restaurants started offering black napkins; vendors thought they were insane), and hung up a wild mélange of monsters, ghouls, and stuffed crows. There were times during the long process of renovation that Mitch felt hopeless, overwhelmed. His drinking increased, and he grew more and more reckless, wiping out on his motorcycle and shattering his right leg just as the restaurant was launching. But in 2002, Mitch, Cyn, Steve, and Kim opened Hell's Kitchen to a nearly full house.

Mitch, Kim, and Steve on opening day at the old location

People loved Hell's Kitchen from the start. It offered the right price point, the right attitude, the right location. Their gospel brunches featured raucous music, extra-spicy bloody marys, and heavily tattooed servers wearing pajamas and negligées. The cuisine wasn't haute. It was hot. Meaty, thick, spicy, and sweet, full of cheese, nuts, sausage, eggs, chocolate, and cream. Right away, Hell's Kitchen became known for its caramel rolls—not only because they were sinfully good (as per Dana's butter-on-cake-style recipe) but because customers got a free one if they dared to come decked out in nightwear as well.

Within a year a line was stretched outside the door each Saturday and Sunday morning when servers opened the doors. Hell's Kitchen served only breakfast and lunch, but this didn't seem to matter. People ate with the gusto typically reserved for nine-course evening meals. Regulars got hooked on various menu items— the rich, sweet Mahnomin Porridge; the dense, smoky, coffee-laced sausage bread; the huevos rancheros piled with black beans, cheese, sour cream, and salsa until it was as high as a cow-

boy hat—with an addictive quality that mirrored the proprietor's own. It was as if Mitch had found the perfect vehicle for his lusty take-it-all approach to life. And diners all over the Twin Cities wanted a bite.

The original Hell's Kitchen

After Jane and Michael Stern visited and posted their gushing review, the mania started to spread. They called Hell's Kitchen peanut butter "the best peanut butter we have ever sampled, anywhere," and orders started pouring in. From Florida, from Iraq, from a certain dreadlocked television host from ABC's *The View*. Cynthia sold her toy business and devoted herself full-time to Hell's Kitchen. The crowds waiting outside grew to the point where they had to institute a pager system to manage the sometimes two-hour wait.

Suddenly, Hell's Kitchen gear—including sweatshirts, t-shirts, and aprons—was in demand. Mitch would vacation and spot people wearing their restaurant brand as far away as Texas and Puerto Rico. Reservations poured in from points around the country from people who had heard about the food in hell and just had to visit when they came to town. Huge groups of Episcopalian priests and city planners and ophthalmologists herded over from the nearby Minneapolis Convention Center. Articles about Hell's Kitchen began appearing in national media. But mostly, their marketing was done by word of mouth.

By 2006, nearly every hour the little cave was operating, people were lining up. There was a throng ready to fill every table when they opened and diners anxious to get the last seating when the restaurant closed at 2 PM. Angry fights were breaking out. People who had counted on getting a table sometimes grew belligerent, like junkies twitching as they waited in line for a fix.

Once, a man who was determined to get a table ahead of others who had been waiting for hours blocked one of the servers as she walked with a loaded tray and demanded to be seated immediately. The situation escalated quickly. The waitress started to drop things and burst into tears. People were shouting. Suddenly, Mitch charged out of the kitchen and—literally—threw the guy out the front door. Under normal circumstances, it would be risky to treat

paying customers this way but not at Hell's Kitchen. And that bozo who tried to strong-arm his way in? He stood outside, sulked for a few minutes, and then reentered and waited quietly for his table. Lesson learned.

In 2007, the partners opened a second Hell's Kitchen in Duluth, a northern Minnesota town known for tourism, bluegrass, and the rocky shore of Lake Superior. They put a full bar into the new location and started serving three meals a day. This gave Mitch the opportunity to develop a dinner menu that included some of his recipes from Rudolph's, New French Café, and Pracna on Main: baby back ribs, Salmon Elise, lobster tacos, and charred sea bass with Jamaican jerk seasoning. Also to partner with his best

Mitch and Steve with their patient wives

friend, Mark "Pappy" Anderson, famed hunter and former schoolteacher—a man who would never dream of living in a place without fir trees, black bears, and wind chills of thirty below.

Now, they were split between two restaurants 150 miles apart, traveling back and forth and getting no sleep. Mitch's demons flared. He started drinking even more—entire bottles of booze by 6 PM, often while he was driving from one location to the other. His spending was out of control, and their expenses were higher than ever. When Cynthia went to pay the bills, it was never enough.

Mitch entered a dual treatment program for alcoholism with concurrent bipolar disorder late that year, spending thirty days away from his family. Cyn—who had decided to quit drinking herself, out of solidarity—shouldered the entire weight of running two restaurants. It was a far cry from the original plan, that she would help out temporarily with Mitch's dream. By day twenty-nine, Cynthia was ragged, but business was raging. Dinner was fast becoming their most profitable meal in Duluth; brunch customers in Minneapolis were making reservations six months ahead.

When Mitch came home, he and Cynthia were supposed to slow down and re-create a sober relationship. Instead, they decided to move the Minneapolis restaurant. Thanks to a growing nationwide recession, they had plenty of options and found the perfect spot, a high-end steakhouse that was dying and desperate to close. The owners offered Mitch and Cyn an incredible deal. They spent three ill-advised sleepless months making the move and nearly clawed each other to death in the process. But they came

The new Hell's Kitchen

out of this dark period closer than ever. And the result, they say, was worth their pain.

In October 2008, Hell's Kitchen reopened in a turnkey fully three times the size of the original space, an 8,000-square-foot subterranean lair in the heart of downtown Minneapolis with the look and feel of an exclusive club from the Prohibition era. Today, Hell's Kitchen has three distinct areas, including a traditional bar, a formal dining room, and an enormous tavern with a stage. Gospel Sunday brunches now feature live music. The servers continue to wear fuzzy slippers with negligées.

And there's *still* a crowd beating down the door.

Cold as Hell

Duluth, Minnesota, is either a bleak, frigid town with chronic unemployment problems . . . or a graceful and historic port city that's home to one of the greatest artist communities in the northern states. It all depends on how you look at it. Mitch and Cyn have always been firmly of the latter point of view.

Their decision to open a restaurant there—on Canal Park, a tongue of land that extends into the icy waters of Lake Superior—was a purely emotional one. Duluth is two and a half hours from Ely, the town where Mitch sequestered himself every time life got tough. It's also about two and a half hours from Minneapolis, making it an easy weekend getaway. It's the place where they keep their forty-eight-foot, two-bedroom boat. Best, it's the place where tides and stars come together, water rushing the rocky shore, the Aurora Borealis arcing overhead at night. When your mind is manic, this is beauty and calm.

During the summer months, when tourists pour into Duluth for events such as the Bayfront Blues Festival, business at HK-North booms. But during the winter (and you have never experienced real winter until you've spent January in Duluth), even Hell's Kitchen echoes emptily. A few groups of skiers and hockey players will wander through. But the city itself is closed down tight. Residents tend not to venture out, and if they do, they're likely former taconite miners living on fixed pensions who want their scrambled eggs, toast, and coffee for $3.99.

It became clear to Cyn and Mitch almost immediately that Duluth would never be the raging money machine Minneapolis had become. But after some soul searching, they decided that was perfectly OK. This was a labor of love. The restaurant employs some fifty people living in a place where jobs are scarce. It's less than two miles from their boat slip. It's populated by people they love. So until it threatens to sink them, they're willing to fund this Hell's Kitchen outpost with proceeds from their Minneapolis location.

Call it a philanthropic endeavor providing homemade peanut butter even when the temperature dips so low it cracks the thermometer's bulb. After all, who more than partially frozen dock workers and dog sled racers need a little slice of hell?

Duluth's Canal Park

Mitch's mom, Annie, one of his biggest fans, visits the restaurant daily and still makes the cookie brittle.

BREAKFAST AND BRUNCH RECIPES

When it came to writing this cookbook, Mitch was encouraged to hold some recipes back ("God knows I tried," says Cyn.). He chose not to do so, because he doesn't do anything "half-assed"—which you no doubt have figured out by now—so what you're holding in your hands is a manual that includes every single ingredient, secret, and cooking tip from the inner sanctum of Hell's Kitchen.

BISON SAUSAGE BREAD   `MAKES 1 (3-POUND) LOAF`

I first started working on this recipe while developing recipes for the Good Earth restaurant in Boulder, Colorado, in 1979. I liked the idea of a dense batter bread, actually, a kind of breakfast meatloaf. The perfect breakfast bread . . . Hell, with eggs, black coffee, and sausage, the perfect breakfast!

10 ounces Maple-Glazed Bison Sausage (see recipe, p. 73)

1 cup firmly packed dark brown sugar

2/3 cup granulated sugar

2 large eggs

2/3 cup brewed dark coffee

2 cups all-purpose flour

2/3 cup dried currants

2/3 cup walnut pieces

3/4 teaspoon baking powder

3/4 teaspoon baking soda

3/4 teaspoon pumpkin pie spice

3/4 teaspoon ground ginger

2 tablespoons unsalted butter, melted

Preheat oven to 350°F.

Place sausage, brown sugar, granulated sugar, eggs, and coffee into the bowl of a stand mixer fitted with a paddle. Mix on low speed until ingredients are just incorporated, about 1 minute. Turn speed to medium, and mix 1 minute more. Add remaining ingredients, and again on low speed, mix until just incorporated. Turn mixer off. Scrape down the sides of the bowl with a rubber spatula. Mix on medium speed another 2 minutes.

Brush an 8 × 4 × 2–inch bread pan with melted butter, and dust with flour. Scrape batter into the bread pan, and place on the center rack of the oven. Bake 1½ hours, or until a toothpick inserted into the center of the loaf comes out clean.

Remove bread from the oven, and let cool to room temperature in the pan. Remove loaf, and wrap securely in plastic wrap. Will keep in the refrigerator up to 2 weeks and in the freezer for up to 6 months.

SCRAMBLED EGGS WITH LOBSTER MAKES 4 SERVINGS

1 tablespoon unsalted butter

12 ounces cold-water lobster tail meat, coarsely chopped (see note)

2 tablespoons heavy cream

8 extra-large eggs

Kosher salt

Ground black pepper

4 teaspoons salmon roe

2 teaspoons minced fresh chives

Melt butter in a large nonstick skillet over high heat. Add lobster pieces, and cook and stir until heated through, about 2 minutes. Reduce heat to medium, and add heavy cream. Cook until hot.

Crack in eggs, and stir continually with a rubber spatula. Season with salt and pepper (see note), and continue cooking until eggs are fluffy and set, about 3 minutes.

Divide between 4 plates, garnish with chives, and spoon 1 teaspoon of the salmon roe over each portion.

NOTE: You can substitute shrimp or crab for the lobster. If using crab, find the best one you can. I like to buy king crab legs and pull the meat into large chunks. It makes for a beautiful presentation, and you get these wonderful sweet and salty profiles.

You can also try adding 2 teaspoons of fresh lemon juice to the scrambled eggs and substituting lemon pepper for the kosher salt and ground black pepper.

Everything You've Ever Wanted to Know about Eggs

Huevos, oefs, or *das ei,* an egg by any other name would taste as sweet. That said, not all eggs you buy at the store are fresh. A simple way to check is to place them in a bowl of cold water; those that float are only good for throwing.

But which came first, the chicken or the egg? Darwin speculated that the chicken egg came from a different species. So since dinosaurs laid eggs long before Bantams ruled the roost, which came first, the chicken or the chicken egg? Is only an egg that hatches into a chicken a chicken egg? Or is only an egg laid by a chicken to be considered a chicken egg? Or is only an egg laid by a chicken that hatches into a chicken a chicken egg?

FRIED EGGS

½ teaspoon unsalted butter

2 extra-large eggs

Kosher or sea salt

Ground black pepper

Melt butter over medium-high heat in a small nonstick skillet until hot and bubbling. Gently crack eggs into the skillet (see note), and reduce temperature to medium. Cook to desired done-

ness (see variations). Season with salt and pepper. Makes 1 serving.

NOTE: Some more cautious cooks will crack their eggs into a small bowl first and then gently pour them into the hot butter.

VARIATIONS

EGGS UP: Cook eggs until whites have set and yolk is warm but runny, about 90 seconds.

OVER EASY: Cook as eggs up, but gently flip eggs over and cook for about another 7 to 9 seconds.

OVER MEDIUM: Cook as over easy, but increase the time after flipping to 9 to 15 seconds.

OVER HARD: Cook as over easy, but really, at this point, it doesn't matter how much longer you cook them, since the only thing the eggs are good for now is composting.

SCRAMBLED EGGS

The key to success here—I believe—is to cook the eggs very slowly. This makes for beautiful, rich, and fluffy eggs.

½ teaspoon unsalted butter

2 extra-large eggs

2 teaspoons heavy cream

Kosher salt

Ground black pepper

Melt butter in a small nonstick skillet over medium heat until warm. Gently crack eggs into butter, and add heavy cream. Cook, stirring continually, with a rubber spatula, about 2 to 2½ minutes. Makes 1 serving.

POACHED EGGS

1½ cups water (see note)

¼ teaspoon kosher salt

2 extra-large eggs

Add water and salt to a small nonstick skillet, and heat to a boil. Reduce heat to simmer. Crack 1 of the eggs into a small bowl, and gently pour egg into simmering water. Repeat for second egg.

Simmer 4½ to 5 minutes. Yolks will turn a hazy pink as they cook. Remove with a slotted spoon, and drain. Proper poaching may take a little practice to perfect. Makes 1 serving.

NOTE: For a little more flavor, poach your eggs in chicken broth, milk, or even heavy cream.

SHIRRED EGGS

Shirred eggs are baked eggs, traditionally cooked in cream. We start ours off in a skillet, then transfer to a ramekin, and finish in the oven.

1 tablespoon heavy cream

2 extra-large eggs

2 teaspoons grated Parmesan cheese

Ground black pepper

Preheat oven to 350°F.

Warm cream in a small nonstick skillet over medium heat until just simmering. Crack in eggs, and cook for about 1 minute. Gently slide eggs into an ovenproof ramekin, and sprinkle Parmesan cheese and ground black pepper over the top.

Place the ramekin on the center rack of the oven, and bake about 5 minutes.

Be careful not to overcook the eggs. The ramekin will retain a lot of heat and continue cooking the eggs well after they have been taken from the oven.

INDIVIDUAL VEGETABLE FRITTATAS `MAKES 4`

> We make these one at a time because they turn out better that way.

8 teaspoons unsalted butter, divided

3 cups assorted coarsely chopped vegetables, divided (see note)

8 teaspoons heavy cream, divided

8 extra-large eggs, divided

1 cup shredded mozzarella cheese (4 ounces), divided

Kosher salt

Ground black pepper

Preheat oven to 200°F.

Melt 2 teaspoons of the butter in a small nonstick skillet over medium-high heat. Add one-quarter of the chopped vegetables, and cook and stir 13 to 15 seconds. You don't want to cook these too much; the vegetables should still be crunchy when served.

Add 2 teaspoons of the heavy cream and heat until warm. Crack 2 of the eggs into skillet, and stir with a rubber spatula until eggs just start to come together. Add ¼ cup of the mozzarella, and stir to mix in well. Stop stirring, and allow eggs to set on the bottom of the skillet, about 1½ to 2 minutes.

Gently flip frittata, and cook another 1½ to 2 minutes. Slide frittata onto a rimmed baking sheet, and place in the warm oven.

Repeat for remaining frittatas.

NOTE: Our vegetable mix varies from season to season. We normally use asparagus tips, broccolini, sweet red onions, red bell peppers, yellow bell peppers, Anaheim peppers, cauliflower, and snow or sugar snap peas. Use whatever suits you, but don't chop the vegetables too small. Larger pieces simply taste better, and they look far more enticing on the plate.

FRENCH TOAST MAKES 4 SERVINGS

5 large eggs

½ cup whole milk

⅓ cup half-and-half

1¼ teaspoons ground ginger

1 teaspoon pure vanilla extract

4 tablespoons (½ stick) unsalted butter

12 slices baguette, cut on a strong bias (about 6 inches long)

4 tablespoons powdered sugar

Whipped butter

Pure maple syrup

Preheat oven to 200°F.

Add eggs, milk, half-and-half, ginger, and vanilla to a large mixing bowl, and whisk vigorously until well blended.

Melt butter in a large skillet over medium-high heat. Dip 3 slices of the baguette into egg mixture, and allow excess liquid to drain.

Place slices in the hot skillet, and cook until golden brown, about 3 to 4 minutes. Turn slices over, and cook another 3 to 4 minutes.

Place slices on a rimmed baking sheet, and keep warm in the oven. Prepare remaining 9 slices.

To serve, fan 3 slices on each plate, and dust generously with powdered sugar. Serve with a side of whipped butter and warm pure maple syrup.

HASH-BROWN POTATOES MAKES 6 SERVINGS

2 large russet potatoes, peeled and shredded on a box grater

3 tablespoons unsalted butter

1 tablespoon peanut oil

Place shredded potatoes in a fine mesh strainer, and rinse under cold running water for 3 to 5 minutes. Let potatoes drain, and then pat dry. Heat butter and peanut oil in a large nonstick skillet over high until just smoking. Add potatoes, and cook undisturbed 7 to 9 minutes, or until crispy and golden brown. Flip potatoes with a spatula, and cook another 3 to 5 minutes. Serve immediately.

VARIATION: For a little stronger flavor, mix ½ cup minced white onion with shredded potatoes before frying.

VARIATION: For creamed hashbrowns, cook shredded potatoes in the skillet with ½ cup heavy cream. These won't get crisp. Cook until potatoes have warmed through and cream has thickened, stirring frequently, about 9 minutes.

RÖSTI POTATOES `MAKES 6 SERVINGS`

Röstis are a Swiss potato course, considered by many to be a national dish, once eaten alone for breakfast. Now, it is an accompaniment to other dishes. Röstis are cooked slowly to achieve their traditional crisp crust and moist interior.

2 large russet potatoes, peeled and shredded on a box grater

¾ cup minced white onion

⅓ cup sliced scallion, both white and green parts

¼ cup finely chopped cooked bacon (about 2 slices)

3 large cloves garlic, minced (2 tablespoons)

2 teaspoons sea salt

2 teaspoons ground black pepper

4 tablespoons (½ stick) unsalted butter

Mix potatoes, onion, scallions, bacon, garlic, salt, and pepper in a large bowl. Melt butter in a large nonstick skillet over medium heat, until warm. Form potato mixture into patties, using 1 cup of the mixture for each. Place as many patties in the skillet as will fit without crowding, and cook undisturbed 15 to 17 minutes, or until golden brown and crisp. Flip patties with a spatula, and continue cooking another 7 to 11 minutes. Hold in a warm (200°F) oven. Repeat with remaining batches of patties. Serve immediately.

VARIATION: For a more flavorful rösti, try cooking potatoes in rendered chicken, duck, or goose fat instead of butter.

VARIATION: For a richer rösti, add ⅓ cup shredded Gruyère and 3 tablespoons heavy cream to the mix. This is by far my favorite way to cook these succulent patties.

HUEVOS RANCHEROS   `MAKES 4 SERVINGS`

I gotta admit I just didn't see this at first. Steve wanted to run huevos rancheros as a special, and I said, "Whatever." Humored the guy. I'd never even heard of huevos being served with hashbrowns, but Steve insisted. I went through every one of my cookbooks and did an on-line search and never saw any kind of potato as an ingredient. But what the hell, creativity, I'm all for it! So we prepped about ten shells the first day and, of course, sold out in about seven minutes. Go Steve!

   Anyway, these days—on Saturdays and Sundays—we serve anywhere from 100 to 130 huevos alone. It is far and away our biggest seller. "Whatever," indeed. They're not difficult to make but require a lot of ingredients and some prep. Believe me, they're well worth the trouble. And if you happen to be at the restaurant and have some huevos, stick your head in the kitchen and say thanks to the little bastard.

4 (6-inch) flour tortillas

1 quart lard or vegetable oil

1 teaspoon granulated garlic

1 large russet potato, peeled and shredded

3 tablespoons unsalted butter

1 teaspoon peanut oil

2 cups Spicy Black Beans (see recipe)

8 large eggs

2 teaspoons unsalted butter

8 teaspoons heavy cream

Kosher salt

Ground black pepper

1⅓ cups shredded pepper jack cheese

1 cup sour cream

1 cup Salsa con Misho (see recipe, p. 146)

Prepare Spicy Black Beans. The recipe calls for dried beans, which means a 4-hour soak and at least 1 hour of cooking time, so plan ahead.

Fill a high-sided cast iron skillet or a large, heavy Dutch oven with 2 inches of lard or vegetable oil, and heat over medium high until it just begins to smoke, about 7 to 9 minutes. While fat heats, poke holes in flour tortillas with a sharp knife or fork to prevent tortillas from separating and forming large bubbles. Place 1 tortilla in bubbling fat, and fry until golden brown, about 5 minutes. Flip and continue frying another 2 to 3 minutes. Remove tortilla with a slotted spoon or tongs. Drain on a double thickness of paper towel, and sprinkle with granulated garlic while still hot. Fry remaining tortillas, dry, and sprinkle with granulated garlic. (See "Mitch's Primer on Deep-Frying," p. 103.)

Warm Spicy Black Beans in a small saucepan over medium heat.

Melt 3 tablespoons butter and peanut oil in a large nonstick skillet over high heat until hot. Add potatoes, reduce heat to medium high, and cook 7 to 9 minutes, or until golden brown. Flip potatoes, and cook another 3 to 5 minutes.

Meanwhile, melt 2 teaspoons butter in a large nonstick skillet over medium heat, and crack in eggs. Add heavy cream, and season with salt and pepper. Stir continually with a rubber spatula until eggs have coagulated and are light and fluffy, about 3½ to 5 minutes. Turn off the heat.

To assemble, place 1 fried tortilla on each of 4 ovenproof plates. Divide hashbrowns, and spread over tortillas. Divide black beans, and spread over hashbrowns. Divide scrambled eggs, and spread over black beans. Divide shredded cheese, and sprinkle over eggs.

Place plates under the broiler, and cook until cheese has melted and is slightly browned, about 3 to 5 minutes. Carefully remove plates from the oven, and place each on a larger plate so they can safely be served.

Place a dollop of the sour cream on each mountain of food. Divide salsa, and spoon over sour cream. *Voila!* Simple as that. Serves 4 to 16, depending on how hungry everyone is.

SPICY BLACK BEANS

1 pound dried black beans

6 cups rich chicken broth or water

¾ cup (1½ sticks) unsalted butter, cut into pieces

¾ cup minced white onion

4 tablespoons Honey-Chipotle Barbecue Sauce (see recipe)

2 tablespoons dark chili powder

2 tablespoons ground cumin

3 large cloves garlic, minced (2 tablespoons)

2 teaspoons crushed red pepper

2 teaspoons sea salt

Sort through dried beans, removing any debris such as small stones. Place beans in a large glass, stainless steel, or ceramic bowl; cover with water; and soak 4 hours, or overnight. Drain and rinse.

Place soaked beans in a large, heavy pot, and pour in 6 cups chicken broth or water, making sure beans are covered by 2 inches. Stir in butter, onion, barbecue sauce, chili powder, cumin, garlic, and crushed red pepper.

Heat to a boil over medium high, stirring continually to prevent beans from scorching on the bottom of the pot. Reduce heat to medium and simmer uncovered, stirring frequently and checking for doneness, until beans are al dente—firm but chewable—about 1 to 1½ hours. Remove beans from the heat, and stir in salt.

Let beans cool to room temperature, and then refrigerate. Makes about 8 cups.

HONEY-CHIPOTLE BARBECUE SAUCE

2 tablespoons peanut oil

⅓ cup honey

1 (7-ounce) can chipotle peppers, with adobo sauce

3 tablespoons balsamic vinegar

⅓ cup Rose's lime juice

¼ cup coarsely chopped cilantro

3 tablespoons coarse-ground mustard

3 large cloves garlic, minced (2 tablespoons)

1 tablespoon ground black pepper

1 tablespoon ground cumin

1 tablespoon kosher salt

Pour peanut oil into a ⅓-cup measure, and pour into a food processor fitted with a steel chopping blade. Measure honey into the same ⅓-cup measure (oil residue will keep honey from sticking).

Add honey, chipotle peppers, adobo sauce, and balsamic vinegar. Process until smooth. Add remaining ingredients, and process until well blended.

Place sauce in a container with a tight-fitting lid and refrigerate. Makes about 3 cups.

GRANOLA `MAKES ABOUT 2 CUPS`

2 cups rolled oats

½ cup slivered almonds

¼ cup firmly packed dark brown sugar

1 teaspoon sea salt

⅛ teaspoon ground cinnamon

3 tablespoons peanut oil

2 tablespoons spun honey (see note)

1 tablespoon granulated sugar

1½ teaspoons pure vanilla extract

Preheat oven to 300°F.

Add oats, slivered almonds, brown sugar, salt, and cinnamon to the bowl of a stand mixer fitted with a paddle. Mix until well blended.

Add peanut oil, honey, and granulated sugar to a small saucepan. Heat to a boil over medium high, stirring continually. Remove the pan from the heat, and stir in vanilla. Pour hot mixture over oat mixture in the stand mixer's bowl, and mix until well incorporated.

Spray a rimmed baking sheet with cooking spray, or brush lightly with peanut oil. Spread granola evenly over greased pan, and place on the center rack of the oven. Bake 15 minutes.

Remove the pan from the oven, and stir mixture with a wooden spoon. Return the pan to the oven, and cook another 15 minutes. Remove the pan, and let cool to room temperature.

Break up granola with your hands, and place it in a container with a tight-fitting lid. Granola does not need to be refrigerated. Makes about 2 cups.

NOTE: I like to use spun honey, which is more of a spread and gives the granola a coarser texture.

BASIC PANCAKE BATTER `MAKES APPROXIMATELY 6 CUPS`

1⅓ cups buttermilk

3 large eggs

1 cup (2 sticks) unsalted butter, melted

⅔ cup whole milk

¼ cup granulated sugar

2 cups Carbon's Golden Malted Pancake and Waffle Flour

¾ cup + 2 tablespoons coarse-ground cornmeal

Add buttermilk, eggs, melted butter, and whole milk to the bowl of a stand mixer fitted with a wire whisk attachment, and mix until blended. Add sugar, Carbon's flour, and cornmeal, and whisk on low speed for 3 minutes. Stop mixer, and scrape down the sides of the bowl with a rubber spatula. Mix batter on medium-high speed for another 3 minutes. Place batter in a container with a tight-fitting lid. Will keep refrigerated for up to 3 days.

BASIC PANCAKE BATTER WITHOUT CARBON'S MALTED FLOUR `MAKES APPROXIMATELY 6 CUPS`

Carbon's Malted Flour is not readily available at retail stores, so I have tried to approximate the recipe here using malted milk powder.

1 cup buttermilk

3 large eggs

1 cup (2 sticks) unsalted butter, melted

¾ cup whole milk

1½ cups all-purpose flour

¾ cup + 2 tablespoons coarse-ground cornmeal

½ cup whole wheat flour

¼ cup malted milk powder

2 tablespoons granulated sugar

4 teaspoons baking powder

½ teaspoon baking soda

½ teaspoon kosher salt

Add buttermilk, eggs, melted butter, and whole milk to the bowl of a stand mixer fitted with a wire whisk attachment, and mix until blended. Sift remaining ingredients into a large bowl. Add flour mixture to buttermilk mixture, and whisk on low speed for 3 minutes. Stop mixer, and scrape down the sides of the bowl with a rubber spatula. Mix batter on medium speed for another 3 minutes. Place batter in a container with a tight-fitting lid. Will keep refrigerated for up to 3 days.

CORNMEAL PANCAKES `MAKES 8 PANCAKES`

2 cups pancake batter (see recipes)

3 tablespoons unsalted butter, melted

Heat a large nonstick or cast iron skillet over medium high. Brush skillet with melted butter, and drop batter into the hot skillet in ¼-cup portions. Leave about 2 inches between pancakes to allow them to spread. Cook until bubbles appear and bottoms are golden brown, about 5 minutes. Flip pancakes, and cook another 2 to 3 minutes. Remove from the skillet, and hold in a warm (200°F) oven. Repeat with remaining batter, wiping the skillet and brushing with fresh melted butter between each batch. Dust pancakes with powdered sugar, and serve immediately with warm pure maple syrup.

OATMEAL `MAKES 4 CUPS`

This ain't your mama's oatmeal. At Hell's Kitchen, we use a combination of steel-cut and rolled oats. Steel-cut oats are whole grain groats—the inner portion of the oat kernel—which have only been cut into 2 or 3 pieces. As such, they take longer to cook than rolled oats. Rolled oats have been rolled into flakes under heavy rollers. I like that the mouth feel of this oatmeal highlights the different textures of the two different kinds of oats.

2½ cups whole milk

1 cup steel-cut oats

1 teaspoon kosher salt

½ cup rolled oats (see note)

⅔ cup warm half-and-half

Brown sugar

Fresh berries

Heat water to a simmer in a saucepan over medium high. Pour milk into a large bowl, and place the bowl over simmering water. Heat milk until it just simmers. Gradually stir in steel-cut oats and salt, and cook, stirring frequently, about 15 minutes. Stir in rolled oats, and cook until all milk is absorbed, about 13 minutes. Just prior to serving, thin oatmeal to desired consistency with warm half-and-half.

To serve, top oatmeal with brown sugar, fresh berries, and any remaining half-and-half. I like adding a dollop of sweet cream butter on the top of mine.

NOTE: When I say rolled oats, I *mean* rolled oats. Don't use quick oats in this recipe. They cook too fast and end up turning the dish to mush.

FRIED OATMEAL   `MAKES 5 SERVINGS`

4 cups Oatmeal (see recipe)

1½ cups all-purpose flour

¾ (1½ sticks) cup unsalted butter, melted

Unsalted butter

Homemade Syrup (see recipe)

> My Aunt Frances showed me this preparation when I was a child, and I've loved it ever since. The patties fry up crisp on the outside, but they're warm and familiar on the inside.

Prepare Oatmeal, using only ⅓ cup half-and-half.

Pour warm oatmeal into an 8 × 4 × 2–inch bread pan lined with plastic wrap, and cover top with more plastic wrap. Place a second 8 × 4 × 2–inch bread pan on top of the oatmeal loaf, and weigh down with two dinner plates. Refrigerate overnight.

Remove from the refrigerator, and cut loaf into 15 slices. Dust both sides of each slice with flour.

Preheat oven to 200°F.

Heat 4 tablespoons of the melted butter in a large nonstick skillet over medium high. When butter begins to bubble, add 5 slices of the oatmeal loaf. Cook slices 7 to 9 minutes, or until golden brown and crispy. Flip slices with a spatula, and cook another 5 to 7 minutes. Remove slices from the skillet, and hold on a rimmed baking sheet in the oven.

The butter browns when cooking each batch, so pour out the used butter and wipe the skillet clean with a paper towel. Heat another 4 tablespoons of the butter, and cook the next 5 slices, holding finished slices in the oven. Wipe the skillet, heat the remaining 4 tablespoons of butter, and cook the remaining 5 slices.

To serve, fan 3 slices of fried oatmeal out on each plate, top with a dollop of soft butter, and pour on Homemade Syrup.

HOMEMADE SYRUP `MAKES 2 CUPS`

This is a childhood recipe: simple syrup, a standard cooking ingredient for everything from baking to cocktails. For my brother, sister, and me, it was the only vehicle we knew to get pancakes, oatmeal, and mush into our mouths. When heated, it goes through several stages of viscosity and hardness, from a thin sweetener to hard crack candy. The old man overcooked this one morning, rendering the mush to taffy. We could lift our plates off the table with just our forks stuck in the syrup.

1½ cups water

1½ cups granulated sugar

½ teaspoon pure vanilla

Add water to a small saucepan over medium-high heat, and whisk in sugar until dissolved. Heat mixture to a boil, whisking continually. Add vanilla. Reduce heat, and cook until syrup has slightly thickened, about 5 to 7 minutes. Remove from heat, and let cool. Place in a container with a tight-fitting lid. Will keep refrigerated for 2 weeks.

MAHNOMIN PORRIDGE `MAKES 4 SERVINGS`

I first got the idea for this recipe more than twenty years ago while reading transcripts of journals kept by fur traders traveling across Canada in the nineteenth century. There was a meal served by Cree Indians that consisted of wild rice with nuts and berries and sweetened with maple syrup. But I decided it needed more fat, so I added heavy cream.

4 cups cooked wild rice

½ cup roasted hazelnuts, cracked

½ cup dried blueberries

¼ cup sweetened dried cranberries (Craisins)

¼ cup pure maple syrup

1 cup heavy whipping cream

Add cooked wild rice, hazelnuts, blueberries, Craisins, and maple syrup to a heavy, nonstick or enameled cast iron saucepan, and cook over medium-high heat for about 3 minutes. Add heavy cream, and stirring continually, heat through, about 2 minutes. Ladle into bowls, and serve immediately.

MAPLE-GLAZED BISON SAUSAGE `MAKES ROUGHLY 8 PATTIES`

1 pound ground bison chuck

⅔ cup dried onion

6 tablespoons pure maple syrup

3 medium cloves garlic, minced (1 tablespoon)

2 teaspoons fennel seed

2 teaspoons fresh thyme

2 teaspoons dried sage

2 teaspoons crushed red pepper

1 teaspoon ground white pepper

1 teaspoon curing salt (see note)

The U.S. Department of Agriculture recommends cooking ground meats to an internal temperature of 160°F. With a product so small and relatively thin, you would be hard-pressed to get an accurate reading using a meat thermometer. With all due respect to the USDA, you're big people. Proceed according to your own preferences and good judgment.

Place all ingredients into the bowl of a stand mixer fitted with a paddle, and mix on low speed until just mixed, about 3 minutes. Do not overmix the ingredients as this will compact the sausage and make for a tougher, dryer product. Moisten your hands, and pat sausage mixture into 3-ounce portions, about the size of a golf ball.

Bison meat is so low in fat that it should be cooked no longer than 4 minutes per side. If broiling, cook patties on a rack set 4 inches from the heat. For stovetop cooking, use a lightly oiled skillet, preferably cast iron, and cook over high heat. Never press down with a spatula on sausages while they cook as this pushes the flavorful juices out of the patties.

NOTE: Curing salt is a combination of salt and sodium nitrite. It assists in the preserving and curing of meats and sausages and helps preserve the natural color of the meats. If you don't have access to curing salts, just substitute sea salt.

NEARLY CLASSIC EGGS BENEDICT

MAKES 4 SERVINGS

There are a few different stories as to the origin of eggs Benedict. My favorite one, which appeared in a 1942 *New Yorker* article, goes like this: In 1894, a massively hungover (that's why I like this story best) Wall Street trader named Lemuel Benedict staggered along the buffet line at the Waldorf Astoria, piling poached eggs and bacon on buttered toast and slathering a "hooker" of hollandaise sauce over it all. If it's true, that Benedict was my kind of guy.

4 (5-ounce) slabs pit ham (see note)

2 English muffins

8 teaspoons unsalted butter

4 Poached Eggs (see recipe, p. 61)

¾ cup Sweet Cream Hollandaise Sauce (see recipe, p. 153)

4 teaspoons minced fresh chives

Prepare Sweet Cream Hollandaise Sauce, and set aside.

Prepare an outdoor grill with hot coals, and set a grill rack 4 inches from the coals (set heat to high if using a gas grill). Place slabs of pit ham above hot coals or a flame. The ham has already been cooked, so you just need to warm it through. Grill approximately 5 minutes on the first side and 3 to 5 minutes on the second side. Barring an open flame, pan fry the ham in a cast iron skillet over medium-high heat.

Toast English muffins. And by that I mean, toast the damn English muffins! Every time I order a Benedict at another restaurant, all I get is warm bread. A properly toasted English muffin should be light brown in the center, and the edges, a dark brown with flecks of black. Butter each muffin with 2 teaspoons of the butter, and place ½ of each muffin on each of 4 plates, buttered side up.

Poach eggs.

Lay a slab of grilled ham on each muffin half, top with a poached egg, and spoon over 3 tablespoons of the sauce. Sprinkle over 1 teaspoon of the chives, and serve immediately.

NOTE: Pit ham has been internally trimmed to remove the bone, while leaving the marbling for flavor. The hams are all natural and have been cooked through via smoking.

BISON BENEDICT   `MAKES 4 SERVINGS`

4 (5-ounce) bison flank steaks

4 tablespoons extra-virgin olive oil

8 teaspoons steak seasoning

4 slices multigrain bread

8 teaspoons unsalted butter

4 Poached Eggs (see recipe, p. 61)

¾ cup Tangerine-Jalapeño Hollandaise Sauce (see recipe, p. 156)

Prepare Tangerine-Jalapeño Hollandaise Sauce, and set aside.

Brush each bison steak all over with 1 tablespoon olive oil, and season with 2 teaspoons steak seasoning, pressing seasoning gently into meat. Let steak warm to room temperature, about 17 minutes.

Prepare an outdoor grill with hot coals, and set a grill rack 4 inches from the coals (set heat to high if using a gas grill). Grill steaks until slightly charred, about 7 to 9 minutes. Flip and cook another 3 to 5 minutes. Steaks should be medium rare, with an internal temperature of 120°F to 130°F. Remove steaks from the heat, and let rest 3 to 5 minutes.

You can also broil the steaks in the oven. Prepare steaks as above, and then adjust the oven rack so that the top of the steaks will be about 4 inches from the broiler's heating element. Turn the oven to broil and high if you have that setting. Lightly grease the broiling pan, and place steaks on the pan. Cooking times will vary greatly depending on the thickness of the steaks, altitude, type of oven, and how hot the broiler runs; cooking times can range from 5 to 17 minutes, so you'll need to pay close attention while the steaks are cooking.

Toast bread, and butter each slice with 2 teaspoons of the butter. Place 1 slice of the bread on each of 4 plates, buttered side up. Slice steaks on a sharp bias against the grain, and fan pieces out over a slice of the bread.

Poach eggs.

Top each steak with a poached egg, and spoon over 3 tablespoons of the sauce. Serve immediately.

VEGETABLE BENEDICT `MAKES 4 SERVINGS`

4 (½-inch thick) slabs peeled eggplant, cut crosswise

4 teaspoons Clarified Butter (see recipe)

2 teaspoons french fry salt (see note)

4 slices sourdough bread

8 teaspoons unsalted butter

4 slices vine-ripened tomato

2 roasted red peppers, cut in half (see method in Roasted Red Pepper Purée, p. 155)

4 Poached Eggs (see recipe, p. 61)

¾ cup Sweet Cream Hollandaise Sauce (see recipe, p. 153)

4 teaspoons minced fresh chives

Prepare Clarified Butter and Sweet Cream Hollandaise Sauce, and set aside.

Prepare an outdoor grill with hot coals, and set a grill rack 4 inches from the coals (set heat to high if using a gas grill).

Lay eggplant slabs on a flat surface, and brush each slab with ½ teaspoon of the clarified butter. Sprinkle with french fry salt. Place eggplant slabs on the grill. The eggplant will take on the smoky aroma of the flame beautifully. Brush tops of slabs with remaining clarified butter. Grill eggplant until grill marks form on the flesh, about 3 to 5 minutes. Flip and cook another 1 to 2 minutes.

Toast bread, and butter each slice with 2 teaspoons of the butter. Place 1 slice of the bread on each of 4 plates, buttered side up. Place tomato slices and red peppers on the grill; these take only a short time to cook, about 9 to 13 seconds per side.

Place a slab of the grilled eggplant on each slice of the toast. Top each with a grilled tomato and a red pepper half.

Poach eggs.

Top each vegetable Benedict with a poached egg, and spoon over 3 tablespoons of the sauce. Sprinkle with chives, and serve immediately.

NOTE: As a substitute for french fry salt, mix together 1 cup kosher salt and 1½ tablespoons dry Ranch dressing mix. Store unused salt mixture in a container with a tight-fitting lid.

CLARIFIED BUTTER

Clarified Butter is butter that has been rendered to separate the milk solids and water from the butterfat. One advantage of clarified butter is that it has a much higher smoke point, so you can cook with it at higher temperatures without browning and burning. Also, without the milk solids, clarified butter can be kept for much longer without going rancid. Typically, it is produced by melting butter and allowing the different components to separate by density. The water evaporates, some solids float to the surface and are skimmed off, and the remainder of the milk solids sink to the bottom of the pan and are left behind when the butterfat is poured off.

1 cup (2 sticks) unsalted butter

Heat butter slowly to a boil in a small saucepan over medium high. Reduce heat, and let butter simmer 3 to 5 minutes, skimming any white foam that rises to the surface. Turn the heat off, and let butter rest 7 to 9 minutes. Slowly pour butterfat through a moistened double thickness of cheesecloth, being careful to leave milk solids in the bottom of the pan. Makes approximately 12 tablespoons.

MUSHROOM BENEDICT `MAKES 4 SERVINGS`

4 large (6-inch) portobello mushrooms, stems removed and caps wiped clean

4 tablespoons olive oil

Kosher salt

Ground black pepper

¾ pound shaved pit ham

3 tablespoons unsalted butter

¼ pound wild mushrooms (morels, shiitakes, or even portobello), coarsely chopped

1 large shallot, minced (about 1½ tablespoons)

2 medium cloves garlic, minced (2 teaspoons)

4 Poached Eggs (see recipe, p. 61)

¾ cup Sweet Cream Hollandaise Sauce (see recipe, p. 153)

Prepare Sweet Cream Hollandaise Sauce, and set aside.

Prepare an outdoor grill with hot coals, and set a grill rack 4 inches from the coals (set heat to high if using a gas grill). Brush both sides of the portobello caps with olive oil, and season lightly with salt and pepper. Grill caps about 3 minutes per side. Remove and set aside on 4 plates, gill side up.

Place shaved ham in a skillet, and cook through over medium heat, stirring continually, about 3 minutes. Divide ham into 4 equal portions, and place each portion on a portobello cap.

Melt butter in the skillet over high heat. Add chopped mushrooms, shallot, and garlic and cook, stirring continually, for 5 minutes. Set aside.

Poach eggs.

Top each Benedict with a poached egg. Fold mushroom mixture into hollandaise sauce, and spoon 3 tablespoons of the sauce over each Benedict. We serve this dish with a side of fresh fruit.

Other Benedict Variations

You may notice that some of these are not true Benedicts. Tough shit. The tenet here is that Benedicts are layered dishes—bread, meat, egg, and sauce. As such, they lend themselves to infinite interpretations. Some of the specials we have done at the restaurant include the following:

- Parmesan-crusted giant shrimp, a poached egg, and sweet pea hollandaise sauce on a grilled English muffin

- The Wellington Benedict—grilled brioche topped with sautéed foie gras, a charbroiled certified Angus beef tenderloin fillet, a poached egg, and black truffle hollandaise sauce with white truffle oil

- A grilled wild Coho salmon fillet on toasted sourdough bread with a poached egg and sweet cream hollandaise sauce, topped with golden pearls of salmon roe and fresh chives

- A fried flour tortilla topped with grilled chorizo sausage, soft scrambled eggs, and ancho chile pepper hollandaise sauce

- Grilled focaccia topped with a charbroiled hot Italian sausage, a slab of provolone cheese, a roasted red pepper, a poached egg, and artichoke-rosemary hollandaise sauce

- Fried brioche (yes, fried) topped with a lemon pepper–crusted seared ahi tuna fillet, a poached egg, and wasabi hollandaise sauce, garnished with fried ginger

- Grilled brioche topped with shaved Black Forest ham and warm baby Brie, a poached egg, and sweet cream hollandaise sauce, garnished with olive oil–fried leeks

- Grilled baguette topped with sautéed duck confit and apples, a poached egg, and roasted garlic cream hollandaise sauce, garnished with fresh chives and slivers of fried garlic

You get the idea. Have fun, be creative. Drink too much, take a hooker to breakfast, and make up your own Benedict.

LEMON-RICOTTA HOTCAKES `MAKES 16 HOTCAKES`

When my wife, Cynthia, patrols the floor of the restaurant, she looks for diners ready to order, then swoops in and insists someone at the table have the Lemon-Ricotta Hotcakes. It's cute, but it kind of hurts in a way. We have dozens of items on the menu that I think are worthy of her overzealousness. But she has a jones for these hotcakes. Come to think of it, after three years in this restaurant, I don't think she's ever ordered anything but the hotcakes.

6 egg whites

9 egg yolks

⅓ cup unsalted butter, melted

½ cup granulated sugar

1 cup whole milk ricotta cheese

4 tablespoons freshly grated lemon zest

1 tablespoon fresh lemon juice

1 teaspoon kosher salt

⅓ cup all-purpose flour

Unsalted butter, melted (for the skillet)

Pour egg whites into the bowl of a stand mixer fitted with a wire whisk attachment, and whisk on high speed until firm peaks form. Reduce the speed to low. Slowly add egg yolks, and then gradually add melted butter. Continue whisking on low speed until well incorporated. Stop the mixer, and add sugar, ricotta, lemon zest, lemon juice, and salt. Whisk on medium speed for 1 minute. Reduce the speed to low, and gradually add flour. Continue mixing for about 1 minute. Stop the mixer, and scrape the sides of the mixing bowl with a rubber spatula. Return the mixer to medium speed, and mix for about 1 minute. Makes about 4 cups.

I find it best to refrigerate the batter for a few hours prior to making the hotcakes. This allows the melted butter to firm up slightly in the mix and keeps the batter from spreading out too thin on a hot griddle. Refrigerated in a covered container, this batter will keep safely for up to 3 days.

To cook hotcakes, heat a large skillet over medium high. Brush skillet with melted butter, and drop batter into the hot skillet in ¼-cup portions. Leave about 2 inches between hotcakes to allow them to spread. Cook until bubbles appear and bottoms are golden brown, about 5 minutes. Flip hotcakes, and cook another 2 to 3 minutes. Remove from the skillet.

I garnish the cooked hotcakes with a handful of fresh blackberries, blueberries, and quartered strawberries, then dust with a vanilla powdered sugar, and serve with a side of butter and warm maple syrup. You can adjust the quantities and ingredients to better suit your personal tastes. That's what good cooking is all about.

CORNED BEEF HASH `MAKES 4 SERVINGS`

1 quart lard or peanut oil

½ pound Russian banana fingerling potatoes, coarsely chopped

French fry salt (see note)

3 tablespoons unsalted butter

1 pound Corned Beef (see recipe, p. 91)

4 ounces celery, coarsely chopped (about 1 cup)

4 ounces white onion, coarsely chopped (about 1 cup)

8 Fried Eggs (see recipe, p. 60)

Fill a deep-sided cast iron skillet or a large, heavy Dutch oven with 2 inches of peanut oil, and heat over medium high, until oil reaches 375°F or just begins to smoke. Carefully place potatoes in bubbling fat with a wire basket or slotted spoon, and fry until golden brown, about 3 minutes. Remove potatoes with the wire basket or slotted spoon. Drain potatoes on a double thickness of paper towel. Season with french fry salt. For best results, cook potatoes shortly before making hash, or they will tend to dry out. (See "Mitch's Primer on Deep-Frying," p. 103.)

Melt butter in a large nonstick or cast iron skillet over medium-high heat. Add fried potatoes and corned beef, and stir with a wooden spoon until well mixed. Add celery and onion, and cook and stir until onions just begin to pale, about 3 minutes. You don't want to overcook the hash; the onions and celery should still be crisp when served.

Divide hash among 4 plates, and top each pile with 2 fried eggs.

NOTE: As a substitute for french fry salt, mix together 1 cup kosher salt and 1½ tablespoons dry Ranch dressing mix. Store unused salt mixture in a container with a tight-fitting lid.

History, Folklore, and Outright Lies

Why is it called corned beef if it didn't originate in Iowa? The term "corned" refers to the large salt crystals used to preserve the meat. I know. I don't get it either. Written record of corned beef dates back to 1621. According to *The Encyclopedia of North American Eating and Drinking Traditions,* the word "hash" (fried odds and ends) came to the English language in the mid-seventeenth century from the old French word *hacher,* meaning to chop.

So corned beef hash probably had its origins as a palatable combination of leftovers. In the nineteenth century, restaurants serving inexpensive meals—precursors to today's diners—became known as hash houses. By the early 1900s corned beef hash was a common menu item in these places.

So why is it that the only corned beef hash we know today comes from the canned food aisle at the grocery store? Thank the Hobbit formally known as Napoleon Bonaparte. In 1795, Boner, as he was lovingly called, directed Nicolas Appert to invent a method of preserving food for military distribution. Appert started to can preserved foods but actually ended up killing those he was supposed to help save. The cans were lined with lead.

At the battle of Waterloo, Napoleon—of layers of cream and puff pastry fame—met in battle against the Seventh Coalition and forces under the charge of England's Duke of Wellington, for whom beef Wellington was named. Of course, they kicked the shit out of Napoleon, and his retreat was known as Boner's Withdrawal. But it's worth mentioning that Sunday, June 18, 1815, has gone down in history as the First Real Food Fight.

CORNED BEEF

MEAT

1 (4-pound) beef brisket

1 lemon, halved

½ cup sea salt

2 tablespoons light brown sugar

2 teaspoons hot paprika

2 teaspoons ground black pepper

3 large cloves garlic, minced
(2 tablespoons)

¼ teaspoon ground cloves

BRINE

2 quarts water

1 quart distilled white vinegar

½ cup sea salt

1 tablespoon curing salt (see note)

1 tablespoon yellow mustard seeds

2 bay leaves, crushed

SIMMERING LIQUID

1 quart warm water

3 medium cloves garlic, minced
(1 tablespoon)

½ teaspoon whole allspice

½ teaspoon yellow mustard seeds

½ teaspoon sea salt

Note that corned beef takes a week to prepare.

TO PREPARE MEAT

Trim some (not all) of the excess fat from brisket, and rub with lemon halves. Mix salt, brown sugar, paprika, black pepper, garlic, and cloves in a bowl.

Rub brisket with salt mixture, and place in a large Dutch oven. Cover and refrigerate at least 8 hours, or overnight. Remove brisket from the refrigerator, and let it come to room temperature.

TO BRINE

Add water, white vinegar, sea salt, curing salt, mustard seeds, and bay leaves to a large saucepan, and heat to a boil. Remove the saucepan from the heat, and pour brine over brisket—it should completely cover meat—and let cool to room temperature. Cover and refrigerate.

Turn brisket over once every day for seven days. After day seven, remove brisket and discard brine. Rinse thoroughly, and cut against the grain into 2-inch-wide slices. Place slices in a large roasting pan.

TO SIMMER AND BAKE

Preheat oven to 350°F.

Add water, garlic, allspice, mustard seeds, and salt to a large saucepan, and heat to a boil. Pour hot liquid over brisket, which should just cover meat. If not, add more water. Cover the roasting pan with aluminum foil, and place on the center rack of the oven. Bake about 3 hours, or until meat shreds easily when pulled.

Remove from the oven, and take off aluminum foil. Let meat cool to room temperature while still in the liquid. Remove corned beef, and pull into shreds. Place pulled corned beef in a container with a tight-fitting lid. Will keep refrigerated for up to 2 weeks.

NOTE: Curing salt is a combination of salt and sodium nitrite. It assists in the preserving and curing of meats and sausages and helps preserve the natural color of the meats.

Every Sunday is Salvation Sunday in Minneapolis, with one or more members of the Twin Cities Community Gospel Choir performing.

Mitch on Saltpeter

This lively little ingredient, once used instead of curing salt in brining corned beef, has a very colorful past and a very restricted present. It was thought, and I feel I can personally attest to this, that food and drink dosed with "blue-stone," as it was called during World War I, caused a diminished sex drive.

Throughout the ages, this substance has been credited with rendering opposing forces, personal enemies, and the occasional assistant coach, well, flaccid. I know that the general consensus during two-a-days at Iowa State was that the coffee "tasted kinda funny." And nobody was out chasing tail in the evenings.

If you mix an equal amount of saltpeter (potassium nitrate) and granulated sugar, the mixture will immediately ignite and caramelize the sugar, creating acrid smoke. A great party trick, or so I thought . . .

In the summer of 1972, I was invited to Iowa State and coach Johnny Majors's football camp. The football players were housed in dorms about fifty yards from the wrestlers to avoid any testosterone-fueled confrontations. But one night, I got a hair up my ass to play a little prank on the acuity-challenged grapplers. I filled a metal garbage can with one and a half pounds saltpeter and one and a half pounds sugar and, in the middle of the night, slipped into their hall and set the can on fire. I expected smoke. What I got was an eight-foot lilac-colored flame that sounded like a jet engine on takeoff.

Christ! I ran like hell back to our dorms and hid under the covers. Sure enough, about twenty minutes later, the sound of fire and police sirens cracked the air. I was sure I had burned the place to the ground. Thankfully, there was only smoke damage, and I think they relocated the wrestlers to another facility . . . in another city. Man, I am the last guy that should be studying science.

It turns out saltpeter is the oxidizing component of gunpowder. It's also used in fertilizer as a source of nitrogen and potassium. About five thousand pounds of this stuff was used in the 1995 Oklahoma City bombing of the Alfred P. Murrah federal building. Its use is now widely restricted . . . except in corned beef.

STEVE'S TITS-UP CRAB CAKES `MAKES 4 CAKES`

Stevie's always made the best crab cakes I've ever had, and I really wanted to feature them on the menu when we decided to put this restaurant together. After our huevos rancheros, this is the most popular regular breakfast item we serve.

½ pound backfin lump crabmeat

4 ounces coarsely chopped shrimp, cooked

1 cup panko bread crumbs (see note, p. 42)

½ cup grated Parmesan cheese (1½ ounces)

¼ cup Homemade Mayonnaise (see recipe, p. 147)

¼ cup minced red bell pepper

¼ cup minced Anaheim pepper

¼ cup minced red onion

½ rib celery, minced

1 tablespoon whole grain mustard

3 medium cloves garlic, minced
(1 tablespoon)

1 large egg

1 teaspoon fresh lemon juice

1 teaspoon Worcestershire sauce

1 teaspoon Tabasco sauce

1 teaspoon Old Bay Seasoning

1 quart peanut oil

4 Poached Eggs (see recipe, p. 61)

Red Pepper Hollandaise (see note; see recipe, p. 154)

Mix together crabmeat, shrimp, bread crumbs, Parmesan, mayonnaise, red pepper, Anaheim pepper, red onion, celery, mustard, garlic, egg, lemon juice, Worcestershire sauce, Tabasco, and Old Bay in a large bowl. Pat mixture into 4 patties, and then roll in more bread crumbs to cover.

Fill a deep-sided cast iron skillet or a large, heavy Dutch oven with 2 inches of peanut oil, and heat over medium high, until oil reaches 375°F or just begins to smoke. Add crab cakes to hot oil one by one, and very slowly. Do not add too many crab cakes to the hot oil, or it will boil over. (See "Mitch's Primer on Deep-Frying," p. 103.)

Fry crab cakes until golden brown, about 5 minutes. The crab cakes normally sink, so it shouldn't be necessary to flip them. If the tops of the crab cakes aren't submerged, however, turn and cook another 2 to 3 minutes. Remove from hot oil, and drain on a double thickness of paper towels. Hold crab cakes in a warm (200°F) oven until you are ready to assemble the meal.

Prepare Poached Eggs.

Place a crab cake on each of 4 plates. Top each cake with a poached egg, and drizzle with hollandaise sauce.

NOTE: For an easy version of Red Pepper Hollandaise, I sometimes use a dry hollandaise mix and then adulterate it with roasted red peppers, heavy cream, and some of our Bottled Hell sauce.

SANDWICHES
AND BURGERS

PARMESAN-CRUSTED GRILLED CHEESE MAKES 4 SANDWICHES

You'll need to cook these in two batches as the sandwiches are very, very LARGE.

8 slices sourdough bread

½ cup (1 stick) unsalted butter, at room temperature

1 cup grated Parmesan cheese (3 ounces)

¼ cup (½ stick) unsalted butter, melted

8 (1-ounce) slices Swiss cheese

8 (1-ounce) slices fontina cheese

8 (1-ounce) slices Vermont white Cheddar cheese

Arrange bread slices on a work surface, and spread each with about 1 tablespoon of the butter. Sprinkle grated Parmesan over buttered slices, and press cheese firmly into bread.

Heat half of the melted butter in a large skillet over medium high, until just bubbling. Place 4 of the bread slices in the skillet, Parmesan-coated side down. Stack 1 slice of the Swiss, fontina, and Cheddar on each. Cook undisturbed 7 to 9 minutes, or until Parmesan is golden brown and sliced cheeses are beginning to soften and warm through. Flip one sandwich side on to another, and remove from the skillet. Set aside. Wipe fat from the skillet, and replace with remaining half of the melted butter. Proceed the same way for second batch of the sandwiches.

Let sandwiches rest for 3 to 5 minutes before serving, allowing cheeses to ooze together and not run out so much when sandwiches are cut.

Louis, King of the Sandwich

In 1983, I had the great fortune to spend time with Louis Szathmary at The Bakery in Chicago. It was a pivotal time in my career. I was looking for answers, and Louis let me hang on to his apron strings for a while and absorb what I could. He had—at the time anyway—the largest collection of handwritten cookery manuscripts, notes, and cookbooks in the country, if not the world. I was awestruck. In his library I found fifteenth-century writings from the court of Catherine de'Medici, peasant journals, and a personal note from the Earl of Sandwich. Yep, *that* Earl of Sandwich.

Though he published several cookbooks, I never thought Louis Szathmary ever really got his

due. He mentored dozens of chefs who went on to lucrative careers and (unlike me) never made an enemy in his life. His wife, Sada, was a gracious host, and his daughter, Barbara, became a great chef on her own. I think of Louis every time I sign my now customary signature (right), which I plagiarized from him (left). I asked for his permission to do so, which he said he was honored to give.

HELL'S KITCHEN HAM AND PEAR CRISP

MAKES 4 SANDWICHES

4 canned pear halves, in heavy syrup

8 slices sourdough bread

1 cup Spiced Butter (see recipe), divided

4 (1½-ounce) slices Swiss cheese

1¼ pounds shaved ham

4 (1½-ounce) slices fontina cheese

Drain pears, slice thin, and set aside.

Arrange bread slices on a work surface, and spread each with a thin layer of the spiced butter, using about half of the butter. Place 1 slice of the Swiss cheese on the buttered side of 4 of the bread slices, and pile one-quarter of the shaved ham on the Swiss slices. Place one-quarter of the pear slices on each ham pile, and top pears with 1 slice of the fontina cheese. Place remaining bread slices on the fontina slices, buttered side down, and gently press down to compress sandwiches. Spread remaining half of the spiced butter on tops and bottoms of the sandwiches.

Heat a large, heavy skillet over medium high. Place sandwiches in the skillet, and cook approximately 7 minutes, or until brown and crisp. Flip sandwiches with a spatula, and cook another 7 minutes.

Cut sandwiches in half on the diagonal.

SPICED BUTTER

1 cup (2 sticks) unsalted butter, softened

2 teaspoons pumpkin pie spice

1 teaspoon ground coriander

1 teaspoon ground ginger

1 teaspoon kosher salt

Combine softened butter, pumpkin pie spice, coriander, ginger, and salt in a small bowl, and whisk until smooth and evenly incorporated. Makes 1 cup.

MITCH'S HELLISHLY GOOD BLT   MAKES 4 SANDWICHES

The BLT is easily one of the best sandwiches on the planet, and everybody has their own way to do it. Thing is, mine's the best. Period. You use the finest ingredients available, and it's easy to do. Start with chewy sourdough or multigrain bread, sweet thick-sliced applewood-smoked Nueske's bacon, vine-ripened tomatoes (heirlooms are soooo overrated), crisp butter lettuce, and homemade mayonnaise. My preference here is to cook the bacon off first and then fry the bread in the bacon grease. Daaaaaaaaaamn! But for something a little less artery hardening, just toast the bread. Jesus, no wonder I had to have a gastric bypass!

12 slices Nueske's thick-sliced applewood-smoked bacon (see note)

8 slices sourdough or multigrain bread

2/3 cup Homemade Mayonnaise (see recipe, p. 147)

12 leaves fresh butter lettuce, rinsed and patted dry

12 slices (about 3 medium) vine-ripened tomatoes

Preheat oven to 375°F.

Prepare Homemade Mayonnaise.

Lay out bacon in a single layer on a rimmed baking sheet, and place on the center rack of the oven. Bake 21 to 25 minutes. Remove from the oven, and drain off grease, reserving for another use (like frying bread slices or potatoes and onions). Turn bacon over, and return to the oven. Bake another 11 to 15 minutes, depending on how crisp you like your bacon. Remove from the oven, and let rest in the pan 5 minutes. Drain grease. Place bacon on a double thickness of paper towels, and blot excess grease with more paper towels.

Toast bread slices (or fry in bacon grease). Lay out toast on a work surface, and spread mayonnaise evenly on each piece. Place 3 leaves of the butter lettuce on 4 pieces of the toast, and fan out 3 slices of the tomatoes on each pile of lettuce leaves. Lay 3 slices of the bacon on top of each set of the tomatoes, and cover each sandwich with one of the remaining pieces of toast. Cut on a strong bias, and serve.

NOTE: We use only Nueske's thick-sliced applewood-smoked bacon, which I think is the finest bacon in the country. I've never found a bacon I thought could even come close. Even the American Culinary Institute named it the best applewood-smoked bacon in America.

Present your food, dammit, don't just serve it. You've labored in the kitchen, using the finest ingredients available, at no small cost, and now comes the time to serve your guests. Give them a show. Cut your sandwiches on a strong bias, and then turn the cut side out, displaying the sweet, meaty layers of bacon, crisp lettuce, and ruby red tomatoes. You won't need anything else on the plate to get their attention.

Mitch's Primer on Deep-Frying

Deep-frying is a method of cooking in which food is totally immersed in extremely hot oil or fat. The operative word here is "fat." Anyway, it is probably the method people misuse most but love best. Because fat conducts heat very well, deep-frying produces foods that are crisp on the outside and warm and moist on the inside.

You grew up on fried foods, so for Christ's sake, learn how to do it properly at home. Don't leave yourself at the mercy of someone like me. The goal is to get the oil or fat hot enough to sear the outside of the food without seeping into the center. This process is well suited for home cooking, and almost anything can be fried.

Contrary to popular belief, frying is not unhealthy—shame on you for giving in to urban myth!—even with the lard I use at the restaurant. And you don't need a store-bought deep-fryer. Most of the ones I've seen don't hold enough fat, and the temperatures vary wildly, which can be disastrous, not in a burn-center-emergency-room kind of way, more a soggy-pile-of-gelatinous-fish kind of way . . .

Alright, I'll admit it can be a little tricky. Too much food in the fryer and it will boil over. If this happens over an open flame, the oil might ignite. This is to be avoided. That said, at all times when frying, keep an open box of baking soda close at hand. Trying to douse a grease fryer with water is simply incendiary, and your running around with your hair on fire will do little to put your guests at ease. If a flare-up occurs, just powder the shit out of it with the soda. It's a mess to clean up, but you'll live to fry another day.

I use a large, high-sided cast iron skillet. I fill it with lard to a depth of about 2 inches, and place it over medium-high heat. The more fat you have, the more constant the temperature will be. Too little fat and the foods cool it down too much. By the time the temperature has recovered, your food won't. You don't need one, but a thermometer can be handy. You want to keep your temperature between 350°F and 375°F. Any hotter and the foods will burn on the outside while remaining cold on the inside.

Fry foods in batches; do not overcrowd the pan. Keep the proper utensls nearby. Most foods will require a wire basket or slotted spoon, which will allow excess fat to drain off before transporting to an area to cool. Drain fried foods on a double layer of paper towels, but they're best eaten about a minute after being removed from the bubbling fat. That's when the crust is set but the interior is at just the right temperature—still hot, but without burning the palate. Allow your fat or oil to cool to room temperature, and strain it through a double thickness of cheesecloth. Place it in a container with a tight-fitting lid, and feel free to reuse it for up to two weeks.

So there it is, an entire novella, just to cook four friggin' fish fillets. Jesus.

THE WALLEYE BLT `MAKES 4 SANDWICHES`

8 slices Nueske's thick-sliced applewood-smoked bacon

1 quart lard or peanut oil

4 (4- to 5-ounce) boneless, skinless walleye fillets

¼ cup fresh lemon juice

¾ cup all-purpose flour

¼ cup cornstarch

3 tablespoons lemon pepper

½ cup whole milk

2 large eggs

½ cup panko bread crumbs (see note, p. 42)

¾ cup grated Parmesan cheese

3 tablespoons cornstarch

French fry salt (see note)

8 slices sourdough or multigrain bread

⅔ cup Tartar Sauce (see recipe, p. 151)

12 leaves fresh butter lettuce, rinsed and patted dry

12 slices (about 3 medium) vine-ripened tomatoes

Preheat oven to 375°F.

Prepare Tartar Sauce.

Lay out bacon in a single layer on a rimmed baking sheet, and place on the center rack of the oven. Bake 21 to 25 minutes. Remove from the oven, and drain off grease (and reserve . . .). Turn bacon over, and return to the oven. Bake another 11 to 15 minutes, depending on how crisp you like your bacon. Remove from the oven, and let rest in the pan 5 minutes. Drain and reserve grease. Place bacon on a double thickness of paper towels, and blot excess grease with more paper towels. Set aside.

Fill a deep-sided cast iron skillet or a large, heavy Dutch oven with 2 inches of lard or peanut oil, and heat over medium high, until oil reaches 375°F or just begins to smoke. (See "Mitch's Primer on Deep-Frying," p. 103.)

While fat heats, place fillets on a plate, and brush both sides with lemon juice. Place flour, cornstarch, and lemon pepper in a large bowl, and mix well. Place milk and eggs in a second large bowl, and beat vigorously. Place bread crumbs, Parmesan, and cornstarch in a third large bowl, and mix together well.

Dredge 1 of the fillets in flour mixture, pressing in mixture gently. Dip into egg mixture, and hold over the bowl, allowing excess moisture to drip down. Place in bread crumb mixture, and scoop some on top, pressing in mixture gently. Turn over, and again scoop some breading on top, pressing in gently. Lay on a rimmed baking sheet lined with parchment paper. Repeat for remaining 3 fillets.

When fat for deep-frying reaches 375°F, carefully place 2 fillets in bubbling fat, and fry until golden brown, about 5 to 7 minutes. Remove with a wire basket or a slotted spoon. Drain on a double thickness of paper towel, and season lightly with french fry salt. Fry remaining 2 fillets, dry, and season.

Toast bread slices (or fry in bacon grease). Lay out toast on a work surface, and spread tartar sauce evenly on each piece. Place 3 leaves of the butter lettuce on 4 pieces of the toast, and fan out 3 slices of the tomatoes on each pile of lettuce leaves. Place 1 deep-fried fillet on each set of the tomatoes, and lay 2 slices of the bacon on top. Cover each sandwich with 1 of the remaining pieces of toast. Cut on a strong bias, and serve.

NOTE: As a substitute for french fry salt, mix together 1 cup kosher salt and 1½ tablespoons dry Ranch dressing mix. Store unused salt mixture in a container with a tight-fitting lid.

TURKEY CLUBHOUSE SANDWICH `MAKES 4 SANDWICHES`

8 slices Nueske's thick-sliced applewood-smoked bacon

12 slices multigrain bread

1⅓ cups Homemade Mayonnaise (see recipe, p. 147)

24 butter lettuce leaves, rinsed and patted dry

12 slices (about 3 medium) vine-ripened tomatoes

12 ounces shaved Baked Brined Turkey Breast (see recipe)

Prepare Baked Brined Turkey Breast (if you're feeling ambitious).

Preheat oven to 375°F.

Prepare Homemade Mayonnaise.

Lay out bacon in a single layer on a rimmed baking sheet, and place on the center rack of the oven. Bake 21 to 25 minutes. Remove from the oven, and drain off grease and reserve. Turn bacon over, and return to the oven. Bake another 11 to 15 minutes, depending on how crisp you like your bacon. Remove from the oven, and let rest in the pan 5 minutes. Drain and reserve grease. Place bacon on a double thickness of paper towels, and blot excess grease with more paper towels. Set aside.

Toast bread, and lay out on a flat work surface. Spread about 4 teaspoons of the mayonnaise on each piece of toast. Place 3 leaves of the butter lettuce on 4 pieces of the toast, and fan out 3 slices of the tomatoes on each pile of lettuce leaves. Lay 2 slices of the bacon on top of each set of the tomatoes, and top each sandwich with another piece of toast. Spread another 4 teaspoons of the mayonnaise on these pieces of toast, and arrange 3 of the remaining lettuce leaves on each sandwich. Top each sandwich with one-quarter of the shaved turkey, and cover with the remaining pieces of toast.

Use 4-inch bamboo or cocktail picks to secure sandwiches. Cut each sandwich into quarters, and serve.

BAKED BRINED TURKEY BREAST

Most of you, I'm assuming, will use store-bought deli meat for this sandwich. But I would love the idea that someone out there, somewhere, is making it with meat from a brined turkey breast. So I'm including instructions.

Brining in a saltwater bath is an excellent way to add flavor and moisture to meat. No need to brine the entire turkey. At Hell's Kitchen we only use breast meat for our sandwiches. We buy boneless breasts, which weigh around five pounds.

1 gallon warm water

1¼ cups french fry salt (see note)

¼ cup granulated sugar

1 (5-pound) boneless turkey breast

4 tablespoons (½ stick) unsalted butter, melted

5 teaspoons poultry seasoning

Pour water into a large pot, and add french fry salt and sugar. Stir vigorously to dissolve. Place turkey in a large bag, and pour in brine. Seal the bag, and place in a baking pan. Refrigerate 8 hours, or overnight. (For a little extra flavor, I use chicken broth instead of water.)

Preheat oven to 325°F.

Remove turkey breast from brine, discard liquid, and pat dry. Brush with melted unsalted butter, and season with chicken or poultry seasoning. Wrap in aluminum foil—or those Reynolds Oven Bags work great. Put on a rimmed baking sheet, and place on the center rack of the oven. Bake 2 hours.

Remove from the oven, and take turkey out of the foil or bag, allowing juices to remain in the pan. Place turkey on the pan, and return to the oven. Baste every 10 minutes, until a thermometer inserted into thickest part of breast reads 165°F to 170°F. Meat will continue to cook slightly once removed from the oven.

Let meat cool to room temperature. Cover and refrigerate 8 hours, or overnight. Once meat has cooled and set completely, shave into paper-thin slices with a sharp serrated knife.

NOTE: As a substitute for french fry salt, mix together 1 cup kosher salt and 1½ tablespoons dry Ranch dressing mix. Store unused salt mixture in a container with a tight-fitting lid.

A Consise and Mostly True History of the Hamburger

Ancient Egyptians were known to eat ground meats as early as 1341 BC, according to hieroglyphs found in the tomb of King Ray "Tutankhamun" Kroc. Actually, hamburger itself is spelled, hieroglyphically, "twisted flax wick, arm, owl, leg, quail chick, mouth, jar stand, vulture, mouth." Man, they had a different word for everything!

In the 1100s, Genghis Khan's Golden Horde would often ride for days without dismounting, placing scraps of lamb and mutton under their saddles to be eaten raw later. If any of you watched *Pink Flamingos* and saw what Divine did with that rib eye, well, you know what I'm talking about . . .

Later, Genghis's grandson, Kublai Khan, invaded Moscow and adapted his grandfather's cuisine, refining the recipe so it used a better cut of meat and served it with other seasonings. He called it steak tartare after the Russian name for the Mongols: Tartars.

In the 1400s, minced beef was popular in Europe, and by the 1600s sailors returning to the German port of Hamburg brought the recipes with them. In the 1700s, it made its way across the ocean and arrived at Ellis Island. You know how it goes:

Give me your tired, your poor,
Your huddled masses yearning to breathe free,
The wretched refuse of your teeming shore,
Send these, the homeless, tempest-tossed to me,
I lift my lamp beside the Golden Arches!

In 1940, Dick and Mac McDonald opened a small restaurant outside Los Angeles, and fifteen years later Ray Kroc bought the brothers out and single-handedly invented corporate-sponsored, free market, trickle-down obesity.

After all of this painstakingly detailed investigative journalism, I also found out that on May 9, 2007, the Wisconsin legislature declared Seymour, Wisconsin, The Home of the Hamburger. What the fuck? Seymour, Wisconsin? Supposedly, "Hamburger" Charley flattened a meatball at the Seymour Fair of 1885 and put it between two slices of bread "to increase portability." 1885. Never mind the Egyptians, Mongols, Russians, and Germans. Hell, it was Germans who founded Seymour in the first place. German meatballs are called Fleisch-Klöschen. "Hamburger" Charlie didn't invent the hamburger; he invented the . . . well, fuck it, he just didn't invent the hamburger. That claim is just a Kroc of shit.

BISON BURGER   `MAKES 4 BURGERS`

In one scene in *Bus Stop*, Marilyn Monroe sits in a diner, playing with two peas on her plate, choosing a favorite.

"There is always something about one that's better than another," she tells her companion. "You can always choose."

And so it is with hamburgers. Nowadays, you can find tuna, Kobe beef, salmon, duck, lamb, and, hell, even vegetables! Anything that can be chopped up can be called "burger." But for me, it's bison. That's my favorite pea. I can always choose.

1¾ pounds cold ground-bison chuck

¼ pound (1 stick) unsalted butter, minced

5 tablespoons minced shallot

3 medium cloves garlic, minced
(1 tablespoon)

4 hamburger buns, cut in half

ABOUT THE BISON Bison is leaner and healthier than chicken but lacks the insulator of fat that beef enjoys, so it tends to dry out quickly. I compensate for this by folding unsalted butter into ground bison chuck. Chuck comes from an area of the bison that is more exercised, giving it a more robust, thick, and hearty flavor. Butter comes from the area of the cow that pretty much gives everything a better flavor.

AND ABOUT THAT BUTTER Yes, it does read "unsalted butter, minced." I do this for a reason. As you mix the butter into the ground chuck, the warmth from your hands will soften the butter. You don't want it to form a paste. Cut cold butter into thin slices, then cut the slices into thin strips and the strips into a fine dice. You get the idea. Refrigerate minced butter prior to mixing.

ABOUT FORMING THE PATTIES As with most foods, the less you handle this the better. Gently mix all the ingredients together; don't compact the burger. And for Christ's sake, don't knead! Form into 4 (½-pound) patties. Don't overwork it. The patties don't need to be portioned into perfect little pucks. Remember, this is essentially ground steak, and it should be treated with the same respect as a prime cut of meat.

ABOUT PREPARATION Nothing beats cooking burgers over an open flame, whether it's wood, charcoal, or gas. But in a pinch, a cast iron skillet will do a fine job. You want your grill or skillet hot to get a nice sear on the meat! For grilling, cook the burgers about 4 inches from the flame. Cooking times will vary depending on thickness. Once the burger is on the grill or skillet, don't touch it. Don't press down on it with a spatula to speed cooking time. This only dries the burger out and won't make it cook any quicker. Be patient, goddamit! And finally, only turn the burger once. Remember, the less you handle it, the better it will be.

ABOUT DONENESS Meat goes from red (raw) to pink (rare) to pink in the center (medium rare) to gray (well done) to black (burnt). Everyone will now tell you to cook hamburgers to an internal temperature of 160°F. Christ! That's well done! Nothing tastier than a dry, gray hamburger where the sweet, flavorful juices have evaporated, the fat has been completely rendered, and any semblance of taste is only a memory. My theory is that vegetarians were all served "properly" cooked meat at some point in their gastronomic quest and simply said, "Fuck this!" When I was growing up, salmonella and food-related illnesses were—or seemed—uncommon. Now, science (and vegans who just want to piss us off) dictate that temperature. OK, be safe. Cook the shit out of your hamburger. At home I take my burgers medium rare, no more than 130°F. This is about 5 minutes on the first side and 2 to 3 minutes on the second side. May God have mercy on my soul.

ABOUT SEASONING Just don't! Never season the burgers prior to grilling, because salt will draw moisture out of the patties. And you shouldn't season the burgers prior to tasting. Take a bite first, and *then* adjust the seasonings. Everything affects the flavor of a burger: the type of meat, fat content, external crust, internal temperature, cooking medium, how long it rests after cooking, time of day, phase of the moon, everything. Just taste the damn thing before you pick up a salt shaker! (Note to idiots: This should be true with all food.) We serve these at the restaurant with the choice of either a sesame or a wild rice bun. I like either grilled and slathered with butter.

VARIATION To make our Barbecue Bison Bacon Burger, we slather our homemade barbecue sauce on a charbroiled bison burger and top it with 2 slices of crisp Nueske's thick-sliced applewood-smoked bacon.

JAMAICAN JERK BURGER `MAKES 4 BURGERS`

4 (½-pound) raw Bison Burger patties (see recipe)

8 teaspoons Wet Jamaican Jerk Seasoning (see recipe, p. 148)

4 thick (3-ounce) slabs pepper jack cheese

4 (2- to 2½-ounce) slabs golden pineapple, peeled and cored (about ¼ inch thick)

8 teaspoons Dry Jamaican Jerk Seasoning (see recipe, p. 149)

4 tablespoons (½ stick) unsalted butter

4 hamburger buns, cut in half

8 crisp butter lettuce leaves

4 thick slices vine-ripened tomato

4 slabs sweet red onion

Prepare Bison Burger patties.

Prepare an outdoor grill with hot coals, and set a grill rack 4 inches from the coals (set heat to high if using a gas grill).

Season one side of each patty with 2 teaspoons of the wet jerk seasoning, and press gently into meat. Let warm to room temperature before cooking.

Place burgers seasoned side down over direct heat, and grill 5 to 7 minutes, or until meat has formed a light crust. Flip burgers and lay 1 slab of the pepper jack cheese on top of each. Continue to cook another 5 to 7 minutes. Remove from the grill and let rest.

Sprinkle each pineapple section with 2 teaspoons of the dry jerk seasoning, and place on the grill seasoned side down. Cook for 2 to 3 minutes. The seasoning should blacken without overcooking the fruit. You still want some crunch to that pineapple!

Spread ½ tablespoon of the butter on each of the 8 bun halves. Grill buttered buns over hot coals, about 1 minute. You can also butter a flattop griddle or heavy skillet and cook the buns over medium-high heat for 2 to 3 minutes.

Place a burger on each bottom half of the toasted buns, and lay a slice of the grilled pineapple on top. Serve each with 2 of the lettuce leaves and 1 slice of the tomato and 1 slab of the red onion.

BARBECUED PULLED-PORK SANDWICH `MAKES 4 SANDWICHES`

This recipe is a unique mix of northern barbecued pork and eastern North Carolina pulled pork, which I am fucking passionate about. The pulled pork doesn't sell too well above the Mason-Dixon Line. Hell, it doesn't sell that well in western North Carolina. But I like the marriage of a classic barbecue sauce mixed with pork cooked primarily in vinegar, sugar, hot sauce, and crushed red pepper. It's time consuming, but I believe the end product is well worth the investment. Hallelujah!

1 (2½-pound) piece of pork butt

⅓ cup Rib Rub (see recipe, p. 150)

4 cups apple cider vinegar

2 tablespoons granulated sugar

2 tablespoons crushed red pepper

2 tablespoons ground black pepper

2 tablespoons Tabasco sauce

1 tablespoon kosher salt

⅔ cup Barbecue Sauce (see recipe, p. 34)

4 hamburger buns, cut in half

4 tablespoons (½ stick) unsalted butter

Prepare Rib Rub.

Choose a pork butt with a thick layer of fat across the top, AND DO NOT TRIM THIS FAT. Deeply score fat in a grid pattern with a sharp knife, about ½ inch deep. Generously apply rib rub, and press firmly into meat. Let pork sit at room temperature for 2 to 3 hours.

Preheat oven to 450°F.

Place a wire rack inside a rimmed baking sheet, put pork butt on the rack, and place on the oven's center rack. Immediately reduce heat to 325°F, and bake approximately 50 to 65 minutes, or until a thermometer inserted in the thickest part of the meat registers 170°F. Remove roast from the oven, and let rest 31 minutes.

Whisk together cider vinegar, sugar, crushed red pepper, black pepper, Tabasco, and salt in a medium mixing bowl. Pour vinegar mixture into a 13 × 9-inch baking pan. Cut pork roast lengthwise into 3 pieces. Arrange meat in the baking pan, and cover with aluminum foil.

Heat oven to 325°F.

Place the pan on the oven's center rack, and cook 35 minutes. Remove and let cool to room temperature uncovered. Cut each piece of meat into 3 slices. Gently pull meat apart using your hands, and place in a medium mixing bowl. Add broth from the baking pan if meat appears dry.

Heat barbecue sauce until hot but not boiling in a small saucepan. Add sauce to pulled pork and mix well. Check consistency; the pork should be moist but not too wet.

Spread ½ tablespoon of the butter on each of the 8 bun halves. Heat a griddle or heavy skillet over medium-high heat, and cook buns about 3 to 5 minutes. Divide barbecued pork among the 4 sandwiches, and serve immediately.

FRENCH DIP   MAKES 4 SANDWICHES

I don't think this recipe can be improved upon, and believe me, I've tried. Most restaurants use sirloin to make their sandwiches. But I find prime rib just tastes better. We use only certified Angus beef and make our au jus from scratch using pan drippings and beef stock. And yes, there is some fat in the meat, as well as the au jus, but as I have stated before, the flavor is in the fat.

1 (2½-pound) prime rib roast

2 tablespoons Kitchen Bouquet

2 tablespoons steak seasoning

2 cups beef broth

4 ciabatta rolls, cut in half

4 tablespoons (½ stick) unsalted butter

Preheat oven to 550°F.

Place roast on a wire rack in a rimmed baking sheet, and let warm to room temperature, about 2 hours. Rub Kitchen Bouquet over the top of roast, and sprinkle with steak seasoning. Gently press seasoning into meat.

Place on the oven's center rack, and immediately reduce heat to 350°F. Bake about 35 to 40 minutes, or until a thermometer inserted into the thickest part of the roast registers no more than 110°F. Remove from the oven, and let cool to room temperature. Remove meat to a plate and cover. Pour pan juices into a container with a tight-fitting lid and refrigerate. Refrigerate 8 hours, or overnight. Shave cold meat into paper-thin slices with a serrated knife.

Heat reserved pan juices and beef broth in a medium saucepan over medium high to make au jus.

Spread ½ tablespoon of the butter on each of the 8 roll halves. Heat a griddle or heavy skillet over medium high, and cook about 3 to 5 minutes.

Place shaved prime rib into hot au jus, and heat thoroughly, about 1 minute. Remove meat from au jus, and place about ½ pound on the bottom half of each roll. Cover with top, and cut in half.

Ladle ⅓ cup of the au jus into 4 saucers, and serve immediately with sandwiches.

CHARRED CHICKEN
BREAST SANDWICH   MAKES 4 SANDWICHES

Let's get something straight right now: chicken skin is good. I've said, ad nauseam, that the flavor is in the fat. And, as we all know, most of the fat in chickens is in the skin. Ergo . . .

Skin-on chicken breasts have the added feature of literally becoming cracklin's when properly grilled. Bonus. So, leave the skin on. I mean it. If you remove the skin, I won't let you make this sandwich. Go home.

Also, chicken breasts will go from absolute perfection to chew toy in a matter of minutes. Be vigilant, and never take your eyes off the meat when grilling.

4 boneless chicken breasts, WITH SKIN

2 tablespoons fresh lemon juice

4 tablespoons chicken seasoning

4 tablespoons (½ stick) unsalted butter

4 wild rice or regular hamburger buns, cut in half

4 tablespoons Chipotle Mayonnaise (see recipe, p. 147)

8 crisp butter lettuce leaves

4 large slices vine-ripened tomato

4 slabs sweet red onion

Prepare Chipotle Mayonnaise.

Prepare an outdoor grill with hot coals, and set a grill rack 4 inches from the coals (set heat to high if using a gas grill).

Lay out chicken breasts skin side up on a rimmed baking sheet. Brush with lemon juice, and sprinkle with chicken seasoning, pressing gently into skin. Let warm to room temperature, about 20 minutes.

Place on the grill directly over coals, skin side down, and grill until skin is dark and crispy, about 7 minutes. The seasoning will blacken the skin . . . it's not as bad as it looks (unless you really do overcook it). Flip and cook another 1 to 2 minutes. The chicken will already have cooked most of the way through, so here is where you need to watch it.

Spread ½ tablespoon of the butter on each of the 8 bun halves. Grill buttered buns over hot coals about 1 minute, or until golden brown.

Spread the bottom of each bun with 1 tablespoon of the chipotle mayonnaise. Lay 2 leaves of the butter lettuce on bun bottoms, and place a chicken breast skin side up on each lettuce pile. Top each sandwich with a tomato slice and a red onion slab, and serve immediately.

RUEBEN SANDWICH   MAKES 4 SANDWICHES

8 thick slices of Caraway Rye Bread (see recipe)

8 tablespoons Thousand Island Dressing (see recipe)

8 thick (2-ounce) slices Swiss cheese

1¾ pounds shaved Corned Beef (see recipe, p. 91)

1 pound Sauerkraut, well drained (see recipe)

½ cup (1 stick) unsalted butter

Bake Caraway Rye Bread and prepare Corned Beef if you're feeling ambitious.

Make Thousand Island Dressing.

Lay slices of caraway rye (a lot of people prefer pumpernickel—I don't) on a large, flat work surface. Spread each slice with 1 tablespoon of Thousand Island dressing (a lot of people prefer Russian dressing—I don't). Lay 1 slice

of Swiss on each slice of bread. Divide shaved corned beef among 4 slices of the bread. Divide sauerkraut among the other 4 slices.

Heat 4 tablespoons of the butter in a large skillet over medium high. Place 2 sauerkraut sandwich halves and 2 corned beef sandwich halves in the skillet, and cook until bread is crusty and golden brown, about 7 to 9 minutes. Remove sandwich halves from the skillet, and place sauerkraut halves on top of corned beef halves. Gently press sandwiches together. Wipe skillet, and repeat with remaining 4 sandwich halves.

Cut sandwiches in half, and serve immediately.

CARAWAY RYE BREAD

SOURDOUGH STARTER

2 tablespoons milk

2 tablespoons water

½ teaspoon dry yeast

½ cup all-purpose flour

2 tablespoons rye flour

1 teaspoon caraway seeds

DOUGH

1 cup warm water (110°F)

1½ teaspoons dry yeast

1 teaspoon caraway seeds

¾ cup all-purpose flour

2½ cups rye flour

Sourdough Starter

1 tablespoon sea salt

½ cup water

FOR THE STARTER Warm milk and water in a small saucepan to 110°F. Pour into a stainless steel, glass, or ceramic bowl, and sprinkle with yeast. Let yeast bloom, 5 to 7 minutes. Add all-purpose flour, rye flour, and caraway seeds, and mix with a wooden spoon. Cover the bowl with a damp cloth, and put in a warm place in the kitchen (I use the oven with only the oven light on). Let starter ferment 17 to 23 hours.

FOR THE DOUGH Add warm water to the bowl of a stand mixer fitted with a dough hook, and sprinkle with yeast. Let yeast bloom, 5 to 7 minutes. Stir gently with a wooden spoon. Add caraway seeds, all-purpose flour, rye flour, sourdough starter, and salt. Mix gently on low speed until ingredients are blended. Stop mixer, remove dough hook, and cover the bowl with a warm, damp cloth. Put bowl in a warm place in the kitchen, and let rise 11 to 17 hours.

Add ½ cup water, and place bowl back on the mixer. Mix on low speed with the dough hook until dough forms a stiff, sticky ball, 5 to 7 minutes. Remove dough from the mixer, and place on a well-floured work surface. Knead until smooth and elastic, adding more all-purpose flour as needed. Cover dough and let rest 15 minutes.

TO BAKE Preheat oven to 400°F.

Butter a 9 × 5 × 3–inch bread pan. Roll dough out to a rectangle about 9 × 5 inches. Tightly roll lengthwise, making a log 9 inches long. Pinch seam, and place loaf seam side down in the buttered bread pan. Make 3 long, diagonal slashes across the top. Cover the pan with a dry dish towel, and let dough double in size, about 1 to 1¼ hours (see note).

Brush top of loaf with water, and place on the center rack of the oven. Bake 45 minutes. Rotate the pan 180 degrees, and bake another 31 to 39 minutes, or until loaf sounds hollow when tapped. Remove the pan from the oven, and let bread cool in the pan 15 minutes. Turn out onto a wire rack, and let cool to room temperature. Slice bread thick for reubens. Makes 1 loaf.

NOTE: Don't overproof the dough! If the yeast is spent prior to cooking, the bread will rise only slightly and then fall in on itself.

THOUSAND ISLAND DRESSING

1 cup Homemade Mayonnaise (see recipe, p. 147)	1 tablespoon granulated sugar
	2 teaspoons dry mustard
¼ cup chili sauce	2 medium cloves garlic, minced (2 teaspoons)
1 large hard-cooked egg, minced	
2 tablespoons sweet pickle relish	1 teaspoon kosher salt
2 tablespoons minced white onion	½ teaspoon ground black pepper

Add all ingredients to a large stainless steel, ceramic, or glass bowl, and whisk vigorously with a wire whip. Place dressing in a container with a tight-fitting lid. Will keep refrigerated for 1 week. Makes about 2 cups.

SAUERKRAUT

1 (2-pound) head green cabbage, cored and cut into ¼-inch strips

2 teaspoons noniodized salt

1 teaspoon sea salt

1 cup distilled water

Place cabbage in a plastic container. Sprinkle with noniodized salt, and mix well. Let rest 15 minutes. Mix again, and let rest 1 hour.

Dissolve sea salt in distilled water, and pour brine over cabbage. Mix well. Seal the plastic container, making sure you have at least 1 inch of clearance between the top of the brined cabbage and the lid.

Store at room temperature for 1 week. Every 2 days, open and skim foam and any harmless white flecks from top of brine. Stir and replace lid.

Pour sauerkraut into a fine mesh strainer. Rinse under cold running water, and press with the back of a spoon or a ladle, draining as much liquid as possible. Transfer to an airtight container, and store in the refrigerator for up to 3 months. Makes about 1 quart.

Mitch on Ruebens

The true history of the Rueben—or Reuben, its spelling being rather arbitrary—is unknown.

One story holds that Rueben Kulakofsky, a grocer from Omaha, Nebraska, invented the sandwich while playing poker in the Blackstone Hotel from around 1920 to 1935. The hotel's owner, Charles Schimmel, a notorious broomcorn's uncle, hit the scoop one day and put the sandwich on his lunch menu. Rueben, a live one, went all-in, holding walking sticks, and Schimmel went all in with bullets and treys. Needless to say, like a blind raise, the sandwich was here to stay.

Other accounts hold that its creator was Arthur Reuben, owner of the once famous Reuben's Delicatessen in New York, who—according to an interview with Craig Claiborne—invented the sandwich in 1914.

Personally, I find all the poker lingo far more colorful, and given that the Earl of Sandwich invented the ham and cheese while playing cards, my money's on Rueben Kay. Sorry Art.

VEGGIE AND CHEESE PANINI `MAKES 4 SANDWICHES`

BRAISED FENNEL BULB

2 fennel bulbs

½ cup rich chicken broth

3 tablespoons fresh lemon juice

2 teaspoons granulated sugar

½ teaspoon kosher salt

GRILLED EGGPLANT

1 medium (1¼-pound) eggplant

4 tablespoons (½ stick) unsalted butter, melted

1 tablespoon lemon pepper

GRILLED PORTOBELLO

2 medium (4-inch) portobello mushrooms

2 tablespoons unsalted butter, melted

Sea salt

Ground black pepper

PANINI

8 slices sourdough bread

¼ cup whole-grain mustard

¼ cup Homemade Mayonnaise (see recipe, p. 147)

4 (1½-ounce) slices fontina cheese

8 slices grilled eggplant

½ cup braised fennel bulb

2 roasted red peppers (see method in Roasted Red Pepper Purée, p. 155)

2 grilled portobello mushroom caps

8 slices vine-ripened tomatoes

4 (½-ounce) slices Swiss cheese

½ cup (1 stick) unsalted butter, room temperature

FOR THE BRAISED FENNEL Cut stalks from fennel bulbs with a sharp knife and discard. Split bulbs down the center, and split each in half again. Remove and discard triangular root core from the base of each quarter. Slice each quarter into ¼-inch strips.

Add chicken broth, lemon juice, sugar, and salt to a medium stainless steel saucepan. Stir to mix well. Heat to a boil over high, and add sliced fennel bulbs. Immediately remove from heat, and let rest in broth for 9 to 11 minutes. Fennel strips should still be firm. Strain through a fine mesh sieve, reserving broth for another use (it makes a wonderful base for soups or sauces).

Rinse fennel strips under cold running water 3 minutes and drain. Pat dry and set aside. Will keep refrigerated for 3 days. Makes about 2 cups.

FOR THE GRILLED EGGPLANT Prepare an outdoor grill with hot coals, and set a grill rack 4 inches from the coals (set heat to high if using a gas grill).

Cut off stem end of eggplant with a sharp knife. Remove skin with a vegetable peeler and discard. Cut eggplant into ½ inch–thick rounds, and lay out on a rimmed baking sheet. Brush both sides of slices with melted butter, and sprinkle both sides with lemon pepper. Eggplant absorbs butter and oil like a sponge and will appear dry shortly after brushing. Resist the urge to add more butter.

Grill eggplant slices over direct heat 1 to 2 minutes, or until grill marks are dark brown. Flip slices, and cook another 1 to 2 minutes. Eggplant goes from sublime to shit in a matter of seconds, so never take your eyes off the grill. Immediately remove from heat, and let cool to room temperature. Set aside.

FOR THE GRILLED PORTOBELLOS Cut the bulbous base from mushrooms' stems, which may still have sterilized earth and part of the mycelium, or root fibers, attached, and discard. Cut stems from caps, and reserve for another use. Gently brush any dirt from top and sides of caps with a dry cloth. Brush caps top and bottom with melted unsalted butter, and season lightly with ground black pepper and sea salt.

Place mushrooms on the grill skin side down, and grill undisturbed 1 to 3 minutes, depending on thickness. Flip and grill the gill side 1 minute. Mushrooms should be slightly charred on the outside but firm. Remove from heat, and let cool to room temperature. Set aside. Will keep refrigerated up to 3 days.

FOR THE PANINIS Prepare the roasted red peppers.

Mix together mustard and mayonnaise in a small bowl. Lay out bread slices on a flat work surface, and spread each slice with 1 tablespoon of the mustard mayonnaise. Lay 1 slice of the fontina on 4 slices of the bread. Place 2 grilled eggplant slices on top of each slice of cheese, and arrange 2 tablespoons of the braised fennel on top of each eggplant stack. Cut roasted red peppers in half, and place 1 pepper half on each pile of fennel. Cut grilled portobellos into thick slices, and arrange half of a sliced mushroom cap on top of each pepper half. Place 2 tomato slices on top of each mushroom pile, and crown each sandwich with 1 slice of the Swiss cheese. Place 1 of the remaining bread slices on each slice of Swiss, and press down slightly to keep sandwiches together. Spread the top of each sandwich with 1 tablespoon of the butter.

Heat a sandwich press or panini maker. Place sandwiches buttered side down, and spread 1 tablespoon of the remaining butter on top of each sandwich. Press down the top plate, and cook sandwiches 7 to 9 minutes, or until golden brown. Remove sandwiches from heat, cut in half, and serve immediately.

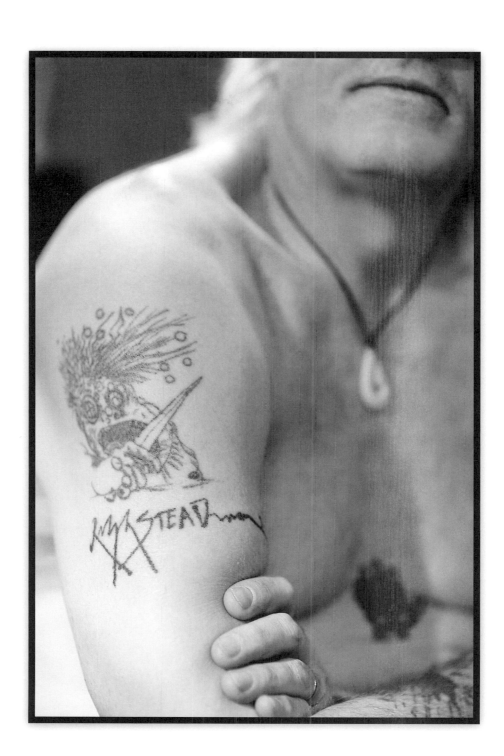

ENTRÉES

SHRIMP LISABETH `MAKES 4 SERVINGS`

I developed this recipe for my sister, who made a wonderful chutney, and I thought a good curry would go well with it. The key here is to make your own pasta. There is absolutely no substitute for good homemade pasta, and it's really not that hard.

And about the shrimp . . . I use large shrimp. You, use large shrimp. Shrimp this size rival lobster in cost. But this is a beautiful dish for any celebration, like Christmas, weddings, anniversaries, or making bail.

SHRIMP

12 colossal (U-8) shrimp, tail on, peeled and deveined (see note)

½ cup Homemade Hot Curry Powder (see recipe, p. 150)

¾ cup (1½ sticks) unsalted butter

¼ cup peanut oil

½ cup Lib's Chutney (see recipe)

1 fresh coconut (see note)

PASTA

5 quarts water

1 tablespoon kosher salt

2 tablespoons olive oil

1 pound Spinach Pasta (see recipe)

4 tablespoons (½ stick) unsalted butter, melted

Libby

Prepare Lib's Chutney.

Place shrimp in a large bowl, and cover with as much curry powder as will adhere. Keep at room temperature at least 2 hours before cooking.

Prepare but do not cook Spinach Pasta.

Heat water, salt, and olive oil in a large pot to a roiling boil.

Meanwhile, warm ¾ cup butter and peanut oil in a large skillet over medium heat. Reduce heat, and add shrimp. The cooler heat and longer cooking time will keep the butter from burning and the curry powder from scorching. It's as close to poaching in butter as you're going to get. Stir in remaining curry powder, and mix well. Stir shrimp occasionally as they simmer; it may take 10 minutes to cook thoroughly. As you would with any food worth eating, keep your eye on it. Overcooked shrimp tastes like undercooked squid, and at these prices, well, that's really expensive squid. If anything, undercook the shrimp slightly—then it's an easy fix, and your guests won't be gnawing on gristle. When shrimp are properly cooked, remove the skillet from the heat, and set aside until pasta has been plated. The skillet should keep the shrimp warm enough.

Slowly add pasta to boiling water so that water does not cease to boil. Fresh pasta takes 1 or 2 minutes to cook, so (again) keep your goddamn eye on it. Cooking times for pasta vary wildly, depending on their size and shape and the temperature of the cooking medium, whether it's water or sauce. Though fresh pasta takes only a short time to cook, you should test it often while it is boiling. The pasta should not taste of any flour and should be firm when bitten.

Remove the pot from the stove when pasta is done, and strain pasta in a fine mesh strainer. Or remove pasta from the pot with a pasta scoop, and allow any excess water to drain off. Place hot pasta in a large bowl with 4 tablespoons melted butter, and toss well.

To serve, divide hot, buttered pasta between 4 plates, mounding it in the center. Arrange 3 shrimp in a pinwheel on each plate, pointing tails outward. Drizzle curried butter from the skillet over shrimp and around pasta. Place 2 tablespoons of the chutney on top of pasta, and shave strips of fresh coconut over the top with a vegetable peeler. Serve *immediately*.

NOTE: Most shellfish are graded by size and number per pound. Hence, U-8 shrimp are 8 to a pound or less (*U* meaning "under"). So the shrimp in this recipe weigh about 2 ounces each, giving you a 6-ounce portion for each meal. Want to really wow them? Serve U-2s!

Since you had to buy the whole coconut anyway just to shave all of 1 ounce over the pasta, do one of two things with the rest: (1) add the coconut milk to the curried butter and shrimp; or (2) make me a coconut cream pie. God, I love coconut cream pie.

SPINACH PASTA

2½ cups + additional all-purpose flour

1 packed cup whole spinach leaves

2 teaspoons crushed red pepper

1 teaspoon kosher salt

2 large eggs

⅓ cup water

2 teaspoons olive oil

Add flour, spinach, crushed red pepper, salt, and eggs to the bowl of a food processor fitted with a steel chopping blade. Cover and pulse until mixture resembles coarse meal (green coarse meal, at that). Slowly add water and oil through the feed tube, with the processor running. Continue running until dough forms a ball. Add additional flour as necessary, until dough pulls cleanly away from the sides of the bowl.

Transfer dough to a lightly floured surface. Cover with a kitchen towel, and let rest 10 minutes. Divide into 4 equal portions. Roll out each portion to form a 12-inch square, and let rest 30 minutes. Place squares on top of each other, and cut into ¼-inch strips. Separate and spread out strips, and let dry at room temperature.

Pasta can be refrigerated for up to 3 days or frozen for 3 weeks. It doesn't work for Shrimp Lisabeth, but for other recipes you can substitute basil for the spinach. Makes 1 pound.

LIB'S CHUTNEY

⅓ cup sliced white onion

6 tablespoons cider vinegar

½ fresh red bell pepper, slivered

2 small cloves garlic, sliced

3 tablespoons light brown sugar

2 tablespoons granulated sugar

1 tablespoon honey

1 teaspoon Sweetened Ginger Purée (see recipe, p. 173)

1 teaspoon sea salt

½ teaspoon crushed red pepper

¼ teaspoon cayenne

¼ teaspoon yellow mustard seeds

⅛ teaspoon cinnamon

2 whole cloves

3 Bosc or Bartlett pears, peeled, cored, and cut into ½-inch chunks

4 apricots, pitted and cut into ¼-inch slices

Prepare Sweetened Ginger Purée.

Add all ingredients, except pears and apricots, to a stainless steel saucepan, and slowly heat to a boil over medium high, stirring frequently. Reduce heat and simmer 35 to 41 minutes, until onions are translucent and mixture has thickened. Fold in cut fruit, and simmer another 11 to 15 minutes. Spoon chutney into sterilized jars, cover tightly, and refrigerate. Will keep for up to 3 months. Makes about 2 cups.

CHARRED SEA BASS `MAKES 4 SERVINGS`

Does this really qualify as a recipe? It's more of a guideline, and a short one. That said, this is my very favorite menu item. Sea bass is sweet like no other fish, and charring the fillet with the spicy jerk seasoning both looks and tastes incredible. Pineapple-Jalapeño Salsa is the only accompaniment fitting for this dish.

4 (7- to 8-ounce) sea bass fillets

2 teaspoons Lemon Oil (see recipe)

2 tablespoons Dry Jamaican Jerk Seasoning (see recipe, p. 149)

¾ cup Pineapple-Jalapeño Salsa (see recipe)

Prepare Lemon Oil and Pineapple-Jalapeño Salsa

Prepare an outdoor grill with hot coals, and set a grill rack 4 inches from the coals (set heat to high if using a gas grill).

Brush tops of fillets with lemon oil. Generously apply jerk seasoning, and gently press into flesh of the fish. Let warm to room temperature, about 23 minutes.

Brush grates of the grill with lemon oil, and place fillets on the grill directly over coals. Grill until seasoning has blackened, about 7 to 9 minutes. Flip fish and cook another 5 to 7 minutes, until center is just warmed through.

Remove fish from the grill, plate, and top each fillet with 3 tablespoons of the salsa.

LEMON OIL

1 cup extra-virgin olive oil
2 whole fresh lemons

Warm oil in a small saucepan over medium heat. Remove the yellow skin of lemons with a vegetable peeler, being careful not to cut into the white pith, which will give the oil a bitter taste. Cut lemon zest into thin strips. Add about three-quarters of the zest to warm oil, and simmer 15 to 19 minutes. You don't want the oil to get too hot since it will start to break down, so lower the heat as needed.

Turn off heat and cover the pan, but don't remove it from the stove. Allow oil to be infused by lemon zest for 2 to 3 hours. Strain oil through a fine mesh sieve, and discard lemon zest. Place remaining zest in a container with a tight-fitting lid. Pour oil into the container, and cover. Will keep for up to 3 months. Makes about 1 cup.

VARIATION: For more complex flavors, consider adding garlic, rosemary, or any number of herbs and spices to your infused oil. Also, don't restrict yourself to using just lemons. Oranges, tangerines, limes, basil, hot peppers, and roasted garlic all make wonderful oils.

PINEAPPLE-JALAPEÑO SALSA

1 cup finely chopped golden pineapple
1 small red onion, finely chopped (½ cup)
1 fresh jalapeño, seeded and minced (4 teaspoons)
1 tablespoon finely chopped red pepper
3 medium cloves garlic, minced (1 tablespoon)
2 teaspoons crushed red pepper
2 teaspoons Sweetened Ginger Purée (see recipe, p. 173)

Prepare Sweetened Ginger Purée.

Add all ingredients to a small glass, ceramic, or stainless steel bowl, and mix thoroughly. Place salsa in a container with a tight-fitting lid. Will keep refrigerated for up to 3 days. Makes 2¼ cups.

NOTE: I don't use any oil or vinegar in this salsa, because I like the flavor crisp and clean. Salsa with oil or vinegar will actually keep much longer, but the pineapple begins to weep, and the red onion, to pale. I suggest making this the day you plan to use it.

MACARONI AND CHEESE MAKES 4 SERVINGS

This is mom's recipe, even though she makes it differently every time. I grew up on it and never realized until I went to college that Kraft made an unremarkable product libelously bearing the same name. This is like comparing having great sex to taking a shower with your socks on.

7 quarts water

2 tablespoons kosher salt

½ cup (1 stick) unsalted butter, divided

1 pound penne pasta

5 tablespoons all-purpose flour

1½ teaspoons dry mustard

¼ teaspoon cayenne

¼ teaspoon garlic powder

2 cups rich chicken broth

1 cup whole milk

1 cup heavy cream

1 cup shredded fontina cheese (4 ounces)

1 cup shredded Vermont white Cheddar cheese (4 ounces)

1 cup shredded Swiss cheese (4 ounces)

½ cup shredded Wisconsin sharp Cheddar cheese (2 ounces)

½ cup crumbled Maytag blue cheese (2 ounces)

1 cup Seasoned Bread Crumbs (see recipe, p. 151)

Preheat oven to 350°F.

Heat water, salt, and 2 tablespoons of the butter in a large pot to a rolling boil. Add pasta, cook for 2 minutes, and remove the pot from heat. Cover with a lid or a kitchen towel, and let rest 6 minutes. Remove the cover, and drain pasta in a colander.

Melt 6 tablespoons of the butter in a large saucepan over medium-high heat. Add flour, dry mustard, cayenne, and garlic powder, and whisk vigorously with a wire whip until flour mixture begins to bubble. Slowly add chicken broth, milk, and cream. Cook and whisk continually about 5 minutes, or until sauce begins to thicken. Add all cheeses, and whisk continually until completely incorporated and sauce thickens. Remove cheese sauce from heat.

Butter 4 ovenproof ramekins or 1 large baking dish. Divide pasta among the ramekins, or pour into the baking dish. Pour sauce evenly over pasta, and sprinkle with bread crumbs. Place the ramekins or the baking dish on the center rack of the oven, and bake 29 to 33 minutes, or until top(s) have just begun to brown.

BAKED RIGATONI `MAKES 4 SERVINGS`

5 quarts water

1 tablespoon kosher salt

2 tablespoons olive oil

1 pound rigatoni

1 pound Hot Italian Sausage (see recipe)

Or

1 pound bulk hot Italian sausage

1 cup Garlic Cream Sauce (see recipe)

3 cups shredded mozzarella cheese (12 ounces), divided

Prepare Garlic Cream Sauce and, if you're feeling ambitious, Hot Italian Sausage.

Preheat oven to 400°F.

Heat water, salt, and olive oil in a large pot to a rolling boil. Slowly add rigatoni so that water does not cease to boil. Cook 3 minutes, and remove the pot from the stove. Cover with a lid or a kitchen towel, and let rest 7 minutes. Drain pasta in a colander.

Heat a large skillet over medium high, and add sausage. Cook while breaking up meat with a wooden spoon, about 5 to 7 minutes. (Most recipes would recommend draining the grease from the sausage, but personally, I like it in there. You choose.) Pour garlic cream sauce into the skillet, and cook and stir until sauce just begins to bubble. Add cooked pasta and 2 cups of the shredded mozzarella, stirring until cheese is melted and well incorporated into sauce.

Butter 4 ovenproof ramekins or 1 large baking dish. Divide rigatoni among the ramekins, or pour into the baking dish. Sprinkle remaining 1 cup of the mozzarella over rigatoni. Place the ramekins or the baking dish on the center rack of the oven. Bake 9 to 11 minutes, or until cheese has melted and browned slightly. Remove the ramekins or the dish from the oven, and let cool slightly before serving.

GARLIC CREAM SAUCE

2 tablespoons unsalted butter

4 medium heads garlic, minced (½ cup)

⅓ cup Velouté Sauce (see recipe)

3¼ cups heavy cream

Prepare Velouté Sauce.

Heat butter in a large saucepan over medium high until bubbling. Add garlic and stir with a wooden spoon. Cook and stir until garlic begins to brown. Add *velouté* and scrape up any garlic that has stuck to the bottom of the pan. Warm sauce, and then add heavy cream. Cook cream until it boils. Reduce heat, and simmer 7 to 11 minutes, or until sauce begins to thicken. Remove the pan from the heat, and let cool to room temperature. Pour sauce into a container with a tight-fitting lid. Will keep refrigerated for up to 1 week. Makes about 4 cups.

VELOUTÉ SAUCE

Velouté is one of the four mother sauces of French cuisine, *espagnole, béchamel,* and *allemande* being the other three. This is a wonderful base for soups and other sauces and should be a part of your repertoire. *Velouté* is the adjective form of *velour,* which means "velvet."

3 tablespoons unsalted butter

3 tablespoons all-purpose flour

2 cups chicken stock

2 tablespoons heavy cream

½ teaspoon kosher salt

½ teaspoon ground black pepper

Melt butter over medium heat in a medium saucepan. Add flour, and cook and whisk continually, about 7 minutes, or until a smooth paste forms. Do not let flour brown. Add chicken stock and heavy cream, and raise temperature to medium high. Cook and whisk continually until sauce just boils. Reduce heat, and simmer and whisk until sauce thickens, about 3 to 5 minutes. Remove the pan from heat, and season with salt and pepper. Let cool to room temperature. Place in a container with a tight-fitting lid. Will keep refrigerated for up to 1 week. Makes 2½ cups.

HOT ITALIAN SAUSAGE

¼ pound pork fatback

¼ cup dry red wine

¼ cup (about ¼ of a large) roasted red pepper (see method in Roasted Red Pepper Purée, p. 155)

2½ pounds coarsely ground pork shoulder

½ cup grated pecorino cheese (1½ ounces)

5 medium cloves garlic, minced (5 teaspoons)

1 tablespoon fennel seed

1 tablespoon crushed red pepper

2 teaspoons kosher salt

2 teaspoons ground black pepper

2 teaspoons minced fresh parsley

Cut fatback into thin (really thin) strips and then into the finest dice that you can. Wrap in plastic wrap, and place in a freezer 2 to 3 hours, or until very firm.

Place dry red wine and roasted red pepper in a food processor fitted with a steel chopping blade, and purée 3 to 5 seconds. Add frozen fatback, and process in 3-second pulses until mixture is well blended but not paste.

Place ground pork shoulder, fatback mixture, pecorino, garlic, fennel seed, crushed red pepper, salt, black pepper, and parsley in the bowl of a stand mixer fitted with a paddle. You can mix this by hand, but it works better in a stand mixer. Mix on low speed until well blended. Place sausage in a stainless steel, glass, or ceramic container with a tight-fitting lid, and refrigerate 4 to 5 hours, allowing flavors to meld. Makes about 3 pounds.

Prime Iowa Pork

Yeah, you can buy a fairly decent Italian sausage at any good butcher shop or grocer, and this recipe makes a very good product, for sure. But I've been around the world, and the best Italian sausage I've ever tasted came from Graziano Brothers in Des Moines, Iowa. Des Moines friggin' Iowa, for God's sake.

Des Moines has always had a very vibrant Little Italy community, and I grew up with a lot of these guys, as did my mom and my grandfather. A few made-men and a really safe haven for outlaws in the 1930s and 1940s (who the hell was going to look for them in Iowa?) just added color

to an already colorful part of town. Trust me, this is the best Italian sausage in the world.

Graziano Brothers
1601 South Union Street
Des Moines, Iowa 50315
515.244.7103

LOBSTER TACOS `MAKES 4 SERVINGS`

1 cup dry white wine

2 tablespoons fresh lemon juice

2 pounds cold-water lobster tail meat, coarsely chopped

⅓ cup unsalted butter, at room temperature

2 cups shredded pepper jack cheese (½ pound)

1 cup packed thinly sliced baby spinach

Kosher salt

Ground black pepper

12 (6-inch) flour tortillas

4 tablespoons (½ stick) unsalted butter, melted

4 teaspoons granulated garlic

1⅓ cups Tomatilla Salsa (see recipe)

Prepare Tomatilla Salsa.

Heat wine and lemon juice in a large skillet to a boil over high, and reduce liquid by about one-quarter, or until about ¾ cup remains. Reduce heat to a simmer, and add lobster meat. The lobster will give off some juices, so simmer until about ½ cup of liquid remains. Add ⅓ cup butter, and whisk vigorously until well incorporated. Add pepper jack cheese and spinach, and stir with a rubber spatula until mixture is thick and creamy, about 3 minutes. Remove from heat, and season with salt and pepper.

Brush flour tortillas with melted butter, and sprinkle with granulated garlic. For service, we place tortillas over a hot grill to just heat through. If you don't have a blazing grill handy, warm buttered tortillas in a hot skillet for 5 to 7 seconds per side. Divide lobster mixture among tortillas, and roll each one up. Place 3 tacos on each of 4 plates, and ladle about ⅓ cup of the tomatilla salsa over each plate of tacos.

TOMATILLA SALSA

⅓ cup finely chopped white onion

5 fresh tomatillas, coarsely chopped

5 tablespoons minced fresh cilantro

2 teaspoons dark molasses

2 teaspoons Worcestershire sauce

2 teaspoons Rose's lime juice

1 fresh jalapeño, seeded and minced

½ teaspoon kosher salt

½ teaspoon ground black pepper

Add onion, tomatillas, 3 tablespoons of the cilantro, molasses, Worcestershire sauce, and Rose's lime juice to a food processor fitted with a steel chopping blade. Process until well blended, about 5 seconds. Stop and scrape the sides of the bowl with a rubber spatula. Purée on high speed until mixture is smooth, about 9 to 11 seconds.

Scrape tomatilla mixture into a glass, ceramic, or stainless steel bowl. Add remaining 2 tablespoons of the cilantro, minced jalapeño, salt, and pepper, and whisk until well blended.

Place salsa in a container with a tight-fitting lid. Will keep refrigerated for up to 3 days. Actually, it will keep longer, but after time, the tomatillas begin to pale like an old pair of jeans. Looks are everything, so serve the salsa soon. Makes about 1⅓ cups.

Kitchen Math

The rule of thumb for most restaurants is to try and bring food costs in between 25 and 30 percent of total operating costs. Then you're making money and giving the customer a fine meal at a fair value. With good, cold-water lobster commanding prices that—as my dad would say—gag a maggot, we are forced to completely disregard these percentages.

So say in this recipe that the 2 pounds of raw lobster meat cost me about $43, give or take. If you also figure in the other raw ingredients' costs, the costs of sides like a starch and a vegetable, labor costs, operating costs, spoilage, and employee theft, then this particular entrée should sell for . . . let me get the calculator . . . uh, $237.31. Like I said, you can't always follow the standard percentages.

BARBECUED BEEF RIBS `MAKES 4 SERVINGS`

8 (1¾- to 2-pound) beef ribs

8 cups cider vinegar

3¼ cups firmly packed dark brown sugar

2 cups Rose's lime juice

2 cups Rib Rub (see recipe, p. 150)

2 cups Barbecue Sauce (see recipe, p. 34)

Preheat oven to 300°F.

Whisk cider vinegar and 2¼ cups of the brown sugar in a large stainless steel, glass, or ceramic mixing bowl, until sugar has dissolved.

Trim ribs of any excess fat (and I mean *excess* . . . leave some). Place ribs meat side down in a large roasting pan, and pour vinegar mixture over ribs. Place pan on the center rack of the oven, and bake 2 hours. Remove the pan from the oven, and let ribs rest 1 hour in vinegar mixture. Remove ribs from the pan, and pat dry.

Whisk lime juice and remaining 1 cup of the brown sugar in a large stainless steel, glass, or ceramic mixing bowl, until sugar has dissolved. Slather each rib with lime juice mixture, and sprinkle generously with rib rub. Refrigerate at least 5 hours, or overnight.

Prepare an outdoor grill with hot coals, and set a grill rack 4 inches from the coals (set heat to high if using a gas grill).

Remove ribs from the refrigerator, and let warm to room temperature, about 2 hours. Brush ribs liberally with barbecue sauce, and place on the grill. The ribs are already cooked, so you just want to heat them through, about 7 to 9 minutes. The sugars from the marinades and the rib rub are going to caramelize on the ribs, so keep an eye on them. It's natural for the ribs to get dark, even slightly blackened, but you want to make sure not to turn these beauties into briquettes.

Remove ribs from the grill, and plate with sides of coleslaw and french fries—at least.

CONDIMENTS, SPICES, AND SAUCES

KETCHUP FROM HELL

3 cups canned crushed tomatoes

½ cup minced white onion

⅓ cup canned pear halves in heavy syrup, drained

3 tablespoons syrup from pears

⅔ cup tomato paste

¼ cup firmly packed light brown sugar

3 tablespoons cider vinegar

1 teaspoon dry mustard

1 medium clove garlic, minced (1 teaspoon)

1 teaspoon kosher salt

1 teaspoon ground white pepper

1 tablespoon mixed whole peppercorns

1 whole bay leaf

2 teaspoons celery seed

1 teaspoon whole allspice

1 teaspoon mace

1 teaspoon whole cloves

Place crushed tomatoes, onion, pear halves, and syrup in a food processor fitted with a steel chopping blade. Pulse until blended, and then scrape down the sides of the bowl. Purée 20 to 30 seconds until smooth. Scrape mixture into the top of a double boiler over simmering water.

Add tomato paste, brown sugar, cider vinegar, dry mustard, garlic, salt, and white pepper, and bring just to a simmer, stirring frequently. Pay attention: with its pulp and sugars the sauce will tend to scorch on the bottom of an unwatched pot.

Wrap whole peppercorns, bay leaf, celery seed, whole allspice, mace, and whole cloves in a cheesecloth, and tie shut with kitchen string to make a bouquet garni. Place bouquet garni in ketchup mixture. Simmer, stirring frequently, 2 to 3 hours, or until sauce is reduced by about 1 cup and has begun to thicken. Check water in the bottom of the boiler every hour to make sure it hasn't evaporated.

Remove the pan from heat, and let sauce cool to room temperature. Remove bouquet garni, squeezing out any excess liquid, and discard. Pour sauce into the bowl of a food processor fitted with a steel chopping blade, and purée for 20 to 30 seconds. Place ketchup in a container with a tight-fitting lid. Will keep refrigerated for up to 2 weeks.

MITCH'S WORLD-FAMOUS PEANUT BUTTER `MAKES ABOUT 4 CUPS`

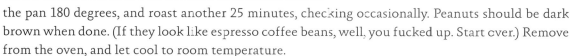

This recipe goes back to my childhood, when one of my favorite sandwiches was peanut butter and honey. With the peanut butter most of the flavor is in the roast; too light and it has no flavor at all, too dark and it tastes acrid.

3 cups salted Spanish peanuts, skins on

6 tablespoons honey

5 tablespoons light brown sugar

2½ teaspoons kosher salt

7 tablespoons peanut oil

5 tablespoons unsalted butter

Preheat oven to 375°F.

Shake peanuts onto a rimmed baking sheet, and place on the center rack of the oven. Roast 25 minutes. Rotate the pan 180 degrees, and roast another 25 minutes, checking occasionally. Peanuts should be dark brown when done. (If they look like espresso coffee beans, well, you fucked up. Start over.) Remove from the oven, and let cool to room temperature.

Place peanuts in a food processor fitted with a steel chopping blade, and process on low until finely ground, about 30 seconds. Do not overblend; you want the peanut butter chunky, not grainy.

Dump ground nuts into the bowl of a stand mixer fitted with a paddle. Add honey, brown sugar, and salt, and blend on low speed until thickened and well mixed, about 1 minute.

Add peanut oil and butter to the food processor, and blend on low until completely emulsified, about 11 seconds. Scrape oil and butter into peanut mixture, and mix on low until smooth and creamy.

Spoon peanut butter into a container with a tight-fitting lid. Will keep at room temperature for up to 4 weeks. After setting for a while, some of the oil may rise to the surface; simply mix this back in before serving.

BLACKBERRY JAM `MAKES ABOUT 4 CUPS`

3 cups fresh blackberries

¾ cup Vanilla Sugar (see recipe, p. 175)

⅓ cup Sweetened Lemon Zest (see recipe)

⅓ cup Sweetened Ginger Purée (see recipe, p. 173)

2 tablespoons unsalted butter

2 teaspoons pectin powder

2 teaspoons calcium water

Prepare Vanilla Sugar, Sweetened Lemon Zest, and Sweetened Ginger Purée.

Heat 2 cups of the blackberries, vanilla sugar, lemon zest, and ginger purée to a boil in a large stainless steel saucepan over medium high, stirring continually. Whisk in pectin powder and calcium water, and continue to boil 1 more minute. Remove from heat, and stir in remaining 1 cup of blackberries. Whisk in butter.

Let cool to room temperature. Whisk vigorously before pouring into a sterilized container with a tight-fitting lid, and refrigerate. Will keep refrigerated for up to 3 weeks.

SWEETENED LEMON ZEST

3 large lemons

¼ cup granulated sugar

Zest lemons, using the smallest slots on a box grater, taking care not to grate the lemons' white pith. Mince zest as fine as possible with a sharp knife. Cut lemons in half, and squeeze juice into a small stainless steel skillet. Add zest and granulated sugar, and stir to mix.

Heat to a boil over medium high, and cook, stirring continually, 7 to 13 minutes, or until zest mixture thickens and liquid evaporates. Let cool to room temperature. Place in a stainless steel, glass, or ceramic container with a tight-fitting lid. Will keep refrigerated for up to 6 weeks, or damn near indefinitely in the freezer. Makes about ½ cup.

ORANGE MARMALADE MAKES ABOUT 4 CUPS

Seville oranges are maybe the finest grown, but they're not readily available. And those beautiful blood oranges are only available in the winter. Just go to the store and get some Valencia or any other large oranges. Tangerines make a great marmalade, but you'll need to use nearly twice as many for this recipe.

4 large oranges

Fresh-squeezed orange juice
(if needed)

1 cup water

2 cups granulated sugar

¼ cup Sweetened Lemon Zest
(see recipe, p. 144)

¼ cup Sweetened Ginger Purée
(see recipe, p. 173)

2 teaspoons pectin powder

2 teaspoons calcium water

Peel rind from oranges with a vegetable peeler. Cut rind into short julienne strips, and set aside. Slice oranges in half and juice them, one by one, until you have 1½ cups of juice. If you come up short, add enough fresh-squeezed orange juice to make up the difference. Reserve any pulp, and add to squeezed juice.

Place water, orange juice, orange zest, sugar, sweetened lemon zest, and ginger purée in a large stainless steel saucepan. Slowly heat orange mixture to a boil over medium high, stirring continually. Reduce heat, and simmer 11 minutes. Whisk in pectin powder and calcium water, and return to a boil. Boil 1 minute, whisking continually. Remove from heat.

Let cool to room temperature. Whisk vigorously before pouring into a sterilized container with a tight-fitting lid, and refrigerate. Will keep refrigerated for up to 3 weeks.

SALSA CON MISHO `MAKES ABOUT 3 1/2 CUPS`

1 cup Peppadew peppers (see note)

2 tablespoons minced chipotle peppers in adobo sauce

¾ cup quartered grape tomatoes

⅓ cup finely diced red onion

⅓ cup finely diced golden pineapple (see note)

⅓ cup finely diced red bell pepper

¼ cup finely chopped cilantro

1 medium head garlic, minced (2½ tablespoons)

2 tablespoons seeded and minced fresh jalapeño

1½ teaspoons ground black pepper

1½ teaspoons kosher salt

1 teaspoon crushed red pepper

1 teaspoon chile oil

Add Peppadew and chipotle peppers to a food processor fitted with a steel chopping blade, and purée, about 5 to 7 seconds, until smooth. Spoon pepper purée into a large bowl, and add remaining ingredients. Stir to mix well. Will keep refrigerated for up to 2 weeks.

NOTE: Peppadew peppers are a piquant pepper available at most grocery stores—one jar will be enough for this recipe. Be sure to save the sweet liquor from the peppers to use in sauces and salad dressings.

Not all pineapples are created equal. Golden pineapples have about twice the sugar content of your run-of-the-mill pineapple, which is great when you're making a salsa with so much heat. As such, they usually command about twice the price but are well worth the investment.

HOMEMADE MAYONNAISE   `MAKES ABOUT 2 CUPS`

2 large eggs, at room temperature

2 teaspoons dry mustard

1 teaspoon kosher salt

1 teaspoon sugar

2 cups peanut oil, divided

2 tablespoons fresh lemon juice

Add eggs, dry mustard, salt, sugar, and ¼ cup of the peanut oil to a food processor fitted with a steel chopping blade. Purée until thoroughly mixed, about 1 minute. Stop processor, and scrape the sides of the bowl with a rubber spatula. Add another ¼ cup of the peanut oil and the fresh lemon juice. Purée again until thoroughly mixed. Stop and scrape the sides of the bowl. Slowly add remaining 1½ cups of the peanut oil, and process until fully emulsified, about 1 minute. Place mayonnaise in a container with a tight-fitting lid. Will keep refrigerated for 3 days.

VARIATION: For chipotle mayonnaise, mix finished mayonnaise with ¾ cup + 1 tablespoon Honey-Chipotle Barbecue Sauce (see recipe, p. 67).

JAMAICAN JERK SEASONING

No, the name does not refer to some village idiot in the Blue Mountains. It was originally a method for preserving and cooking pork. The meaning of "jerk" has been lost over the centuries. It's believed to have gone back to the Arawaks, who traded with pirates bringing spices from around the world.

There are three key spices in any jerk seasoning: Jamaican pimento (which we call allspice), thyme, and Scotch bonnet peppers, so hot they have been known to spontaneously combust. No longer relegated just to pork, jerk seasoning is used on every manner of meat and fish, as is seen in this book's charred sea bass recipe.

WET JERK SEASONING

2 bunches (12 to 16) scallions, coarsely chopped

½ cup firmly packed light brown sugar

4 Scotch bonnet peppers, minced (see note)

8 medium cloves garlic

5 tablespoons ground allspice

3 tablespoons dried thyme

2 tablespoons grated fresh ginger

2 tablespoons peanut oil

2 tablespoons white distilled vinegar

2 tablespoons pineapple juice

1 tablespoon dark molasses

2 teaspoons kosher salt

1 teaspoon crushed red pepper

1 teaspoon ground nutmeg

1 teaspoon ground cinnamon

2 large limes, juiced

Place all ingredients in a food processor fitted with a steel chopping blade. Process mixture until smooth, 11 to 15 seconds. If mixture appears too dry, add more lime juice. Place in a stainless steel, glass, or ceramic container with a tight-fitting lid and refrigerate. Will keep refrigerated up to 3 weeks. Makes about 3 cups.

NOTE: When using wet jerk marinade, make shallow slits in the meat and rub marinade into them. Allow the meat to marinate at least 5 hours, or overnight. For hamburger the slits aren't necessary but overnight curing is.

Scotch bonnet peppers enjoy one of the highest Scoville ratings in the world. Named after American chemist Wilbur "Gawdam This Is Hot" Scoville, the Scoville scale measures the hotness, or piquancy, of peppers, which is related to the amount of capsaicin present. To give you a quick overview, bell peppers have a Scoville rating of 0, jalapeños have ratings that range from 2,500 to 8,000, and Scotch bonnets have Scoville ratings that range from 100,000 to 350,000.

The pepper spray that police administer just because you didn't stop when you saw them behind you because you were speeding but couldn't stop because you had to pee really bad, and when you finally did stop, you ran into the bathroom at the Super America but didn't have time to lock the door on the stall, so the policeman sprayed you right there in the john, and you fell over and peed yourself anyway, thrashing around on that gross bathroom floor. Oh, yeah. That pepper spray has a Scoville rating of 5,300,000!

Also, wear gloves when handling these peppers! The oils will burn your hands for hours if you don't protect them. Guys, do *not* handle these peppers then go to the bathroom. Those boys will be on fire, not in a good way, for what seems an eternity. After doing this three or four times, I've learned to be very careful.

DRY JERK SEASONING

2 tablespoons onion powder

1 tablespoon dried thyme

1 tablespoon ground allspice

1 tablespoon garlic powder

2 teaspoons crushed red pepper

2 teaspoons ground black pepper

2 teaspoons granulated sugar

1 teaspoon grated nutmeg

1 teaspoon ground cinnamon

1 teaspoon cayenne

1 teaspoon kosher salt

Mix together all ingredients in a bowl. Store in a stainless steel, glass, or ceramic container with a tight-fitting lid. Makes about ½ cup.

HOMEMADE HOT CURRY POWDER `MAKES ABOUT 3/4 CUP`

3 tablespoons cumin seeds

2 tablespoons coriander seeds

2 teaspoons fennel seeds

1 teaspoon yellow mustard seeds

1 teaspoon fenugreek seeds

1 teaspoon ground black pepper

1 tablespoon crushed red pepper

3 whole cloves

2 tablespoons ground turmeric

2 teaspoons ground cinnamon

2 teaspoons ground ginger

Add cumin, coriander, fennel, mustard, and fenugreek seeds to a large skillet over medium heat. Cook, stirring continually, until seeds are aromatic and darkly toasted, about 13 minutes. Remove from heat, and let cool to room temperature.

Place toasted seeds and remaining ingredients in a spice grinder, and grind into coarse powder, about 9 to 13 seconds. Store mixture in an airtight stainless steel, glass, or ceramic container, and place in a cool, dry place.

RIB RUB `MAKES ABOUT 2 1/3 CUPS`

¾ cup hot paprika

¼ cup ground black pepper

¼ cup dark chili powder

¼ cup ground cumin

¼ cup granulated garlic

¼ cup granulated sugar

¼ cup firmly packed dark brown sugar

2 tablespoons cayenne

Mix all ingredients in a medium mixing bowl. Place rib rub in a stainless steel, glass, or ceramic container with a tight-fitting lid. Will keep damn near indefinitely.

SEASONED BREAD CRUMBS `MAKES ABOUT 4 CUPS`

3 tablespoons unsalted butter

2 cups panko bread crumbs (see note, p. 42)

2/3 cup chopped walnuts

1/3 cup dried onion, minced

5 tablespoons chopped fresh parsley

3 dashes Tabasco sauce

Melt butter in a large skillet over medium-high heat. Add remaining ingredients, and cook, stirring continually, until bread crumbs and dried onions are golden brown, about 3 to 5 minutes. Remove from heat, and let cool to room temperature. Store in a container with a tight-fitting lid at room temperature. Will keep for up to 5 weeks.

TARTAR SAUCE `MAKES ABOUT 2 CUPS`

1 cup minced scallions, both white and green parts

1/2 cup Miracle Whip

1/4 cup minced fresh chives

2 tablespoons lemon pepper

4 teaspoons fresh lemon juice

1 fresh jalapeño, seeded and minced

Whisk together all ingredients in a large stainless steel, glass, or ceramic bowl. Will keep refrigerated for up to 2 weeks.

HOMEMADE STEAK SAUCE   `MAKES ABOUT 1 1/4 CUP`

⅓ cup unsalted butter

¼ cup minced shiitake mushroom caps

⅓ cup rich veal stock

3 tablespoons Worcestershire sauce

2 tablespoons Ketchup from Hell (see recipe, p. 142)

2 tablespoons balsamic vinegar

2 tablespoons Tabasco sauce

2 tablespoons light brown sugar

2 tablespoons minced fresh basil

1 tablespoon ground black pepper

1 tablespoon sea salt

Melt butter in a medium saucepan over high heat until bubbling. Add minced shiitakes and cook, stirring continually, until mushrooms begin to brown, about 5 minutes. Add remaining ingredients, and heat to a boil. Reduce heat to a simmer, and stir continually 7 to 11 minutes, or until sauce begins to thicken.

Remove from heat, and strain sauce through a fine mesh strainer. Press down on solids with a rubber spatula or the back of a ladle to extract as much sauce as possible. Discard solids. Let sauce cool to room temperature, and place in a container with a tight-fitting lid. Will keep refrigerated for 2 weeks.

To serve, warm sauce in a small saucepan over medium high, whisking vigorously to emulsify butter.

SWEET CREAM HOLLANDAISE SAUCE `MAKES ABOUT 1 2/3 CUP`

Hollandaise is a French sauce that was named, it is believed, because it mimicked a Dutch sauce. This classic sauce takes a little finesse to prepare well. Properly made, it should be smooth and creamy. I find traditional hollandaise a little cloying, however, so ours adds heavy cream, which also gives it a lighter color and, in my opinion, a better presentation on the plate. Though these hollandaise sauces mostly fall under our breakfast and brunch menus, they are not relegated simply to topping poached eggs. All can be used in various recipes to be served with red meat, game, chicken, fish, and vegetables. Use your imagination.

4 large egg yolks

1 tablespoon + 1 teaspoon fresh lemon juice

1 cup (2 sticks) unsalted butter

½ teaspoon kosher salt

¼ teaspoon ground black pepper

⅛ teaspoon cayenne

¼ to ⅓ cup warm heavy cream

Separate egg yolks into a small bowl, and let yolks warm to room temperature. Reserve whites for a different use.

Heat butter to a simmer in a small saucepan over medium high. Gently warm heavy cream in another small saucepan. Do not let boil.

Fill a medium saucepan one-quarter full of water, and heat to a simmer. Place a large stainless steel bowl over the saucepan, being careful not to let the bowl touch the water. If you do, the eggs will curdle and scramble. Add egg yolks and lemon juice, and whisk vigorously. Continue whisking as you slowly drizzle in hot butter. Whisk until sauce has thickened and doubled in volume.

Remove the bowl from heat, and whisk in salt, black pepper, and cayenne. Adjust seasoning if necessary. Whisk in warm heavy cream, until sauce is lighter but still thick enough to coat the back of a spoon without separating. Strain sauce through a fine mesh sieve, in case any of the egg has curdled. Keep sauce warm through service, without cooking. We hold our hollandaise at the restaurant in a low-temperature bain marie. You can use a small thermos at home.

Hollandaise sauce should be held for no more than 1½ hours. If your hollandaise sauce gets too warm while making, or holding, the sauce will break, causing the egg and fat to separate. Once made, hold the sauce in a warm area, away from direct heat, and whisk vigorously prior to serving. Should the sauce break, remove from the heat immediately, add an ice cube to the sauce, and whisk vigorously. The hollandaise can usually be saved in this way.

RED PEPPER HOLLANDAISE SAUCE `MAKES ABOUT 2 CUPS`

Never, ever buy roasted peppers in a jar. It's ridiculous. They can easily be made at home, and the added flavor is well worth the time and effort. Most people believe peppers should be peeled, as we will do here. But in all honesty, if you don't char the peppers and simply oven roast them, once the peppers are puréed, a little bit of skin will not detract from the recipe. Red pepper purée can also be used to enliven soups, sauces, appetizers, salads . . . the list is endless. Also, don't be confined to using only red peppers. Green, yellow, Anaheim, poblano—any pepper can be utilized in this manner.

½ cup Roasted Red Pepper Purée (see recipe)
1½ cups Sweet Cream Hollandaise Sauce (see recipe, p. 153)

Prepare Roasted Red Pepper Purée before making hollandaise. Then, simply fold red pepper purée into hollandaise.

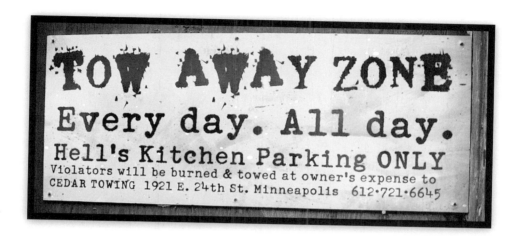

ROASTED RED PEPPER PURÉE

2 large red bell peppers

2 teaspoons peanut oil

3 teaspoons kosher salt

1 teaspoon crushed red pepper

Preheat broiler to high.

Cut stems out of peppers, and slice each in half lengthwise and then in half again. Remove seeds and membranes, and place pepper quarters skin side up on a rimmed baking sheet. Brush with peanut oil, and place in the oven on the highest rack, 4 inches from the broiler elements or fire.

Don't leave the oven unattended; peppers can go from being roasted to being charred in a matter of minutes. Roast until skin blackens, about 7 to 11 minutes. If blackening unevenly, rotate the pan 180 degrees after 5 minutes. When evenly charred, remove the pan from the oven, and place peppers in a plastic or paper bag and seal 10 minutes. The peppers will steam, making removal of the skins easier. Remove from the bag, and gently scrape away skin with a sharp knife. This will be more difficult on the tender areas. Don't worry about getting every last bit of skin.

Place in a food processor fitted with a steel chopping blade, and process 5 to 7 seconds. Add salt and crushed red pepper, and then process again another 5 to 7 seconds. Place purée in a stainless steel, glass, or ceramic container with a tight-fitting lid. Will keep refrigerated for up to 3 days. Makes about 2½ cups.

TANGERINE-JALAPEÑO
HOLLANDAISE SAUCE `MAKES ABOUT 2 CUPS`

5 fresh tangerines

2 teaspoons granulated sugar

2 to 3 fresh jalapeños, seeded and minced (3 tablespoons)

1½ cups Sweet Cream Hollandaise Sauce (see recipe, p. 153)

Zest tangerines using the smallest slots on a box grater or a microplane. Mince zest as fine as possible with a sharp knife. Cut tangerines in half, and squeeze juice into a small saucepan. Add zest and sugar, and stir to mix together. Heat tangerine mixture to a boil over medium high, and cook, stirring continually, 5 to 9 minutes, or until mixture thickens and about 3 tablespoons remain.

Prepare Sweet Cream Hollandaise Sauce.

Fold tangerine reduction and jalapeños into hollandaise.

BLACK TRUFFLE
HOLLANDAISE SAUCE `MAKES ABOUT 2 CUPS`

Truffles are among the most expensive foods in the world and can command prices of up to one thousand dollars a pound and more. But they're so worth it. Périgord, the winter black truffle, is the most well-known truffle in the world, called the queen of truffles. White truffles, my favorite by a long shot, come from the Piedmont area of Italy. The best potatoes in the world, IMHO, are oven-roasted spuds with coarsely chopped fresh white truffles.

¼ cup fresh black truffles, minced (see note)

¼ cup white truffle oil

1½ cups Sweet Cream Hollandaise Sauce (see recipe, p. 153)

Prepare Sweet Cream Hollandaise Sauce, and then fold in minced black truffles and white truffle oil.

NOTE: You can substitute canned black truffle peelings for the fresh, if you must.

WILD MUSHROOM HOLLANDAISE SAUCE `MAKES ABOUT 2 CUPS`

⅓ cup rich chicken broth

1 ounce dried morel mushrooms

¼ cup (½ stick) unsalted butter

⅓ cup thinly sliced fresh shiitake mushroom caps

1 large shallot, minced

1 medium clove garlic, minced (1 teaspoon)

1¼ cups Sweet Cream Hollandaise Sauce (see recipe, p. 153)

Prepare Sweet Cream Hollandaise Sauce.

Heat chicken broth to a simmer in a small skillet over medium high. Add dried morels, and simmer 5 to 7 minutes. Remove the skillet from heat, and drain in a fine mesh sieve, reserving broth. Rinse under cold running water 2 to 3 minutes. Drain and pat dry. Coarsely chop morels. Strain reserved broth through a double thickness of cheesecloth, and set aside.

Melt butter in a medium skillet over high heat. Add reconstituted morels, shiitakes, shallot, and garlic. Cook and stir about 3 minutes. Spoon mushroom mixture into hollandaise. Deglaze the skillet with reserved broth, and reduce until only 3 tablespoons remain. Pour reduced broth into hollandaise, and stir to mix well.

SWEET PEA HOLLANDAISE SAUCE

MAKES ABOUT 2 CUPS

Maybe my favorite sauce here. It is sweet, beautiful to look at, and even better to eat. This sauce—almost anything with peas—goes remarkably well with anything containing Parmesan cheese, so I developed this sauce to go with our Parmesan-Crusted Shrimp Benedict.

1 cup rich chicken broth

1 cup fresh shelled peas (see note)

1 large clove garlic, minced (2 teaspoons)

Kosher salt

Ground black pepper

1¼ cups Sweet Cream Hollandaise Sauce (see recipe, p. 153)

Prepare Sweet Cream Hollandaise Sauce.

Heat chicken broth to a boil in a medium saucepan over high. Add peas and minced garlic, and simmer until peas are just cooked through, about 2 to 3 minutes. Drain pea mixture in a fine mesh sieve, reserving broth for another use.

Spoon pea mixture into a food processor fitted with a steel chopping blade, and pulse 3 to 5 times, or until mixture is chopped but not puréed into a paste. Fold into hollandaise sauce, and season with salt and pepper.

NOTE: Fresh peas are preferred; frozen are a sloppy second. But if you even consider using canned peas . . . I mean, what the hell? Canned peas are banned in seven states! Don't use them. Ever!

LEMON HOLLANDAISE SAUCE `MAKES ABOUT 2 CUPS`

1⅓ cups Sweet Cream Hollandaise Sauce (see recipe, p. 153)

7 tablespoons fresh lemon juice

4 tablespoons Sweetened Lemon Zest (see recipe, p. 144)

1 tablespoon + 1 teaspoon lemon pepper

Prepare Sweet Cream Hollandaise Sauce, and then simply mix together all ingredients until well blended.

BAKED

GOODS

ANGEL FOOD CAKE WITH GINGER-TARRAGON BERRIES

MAKES 8 SERVINGS

1 cup cake flour (4 ounces)

12 ounces granulated sugar

12 egg whites

1 teaspoon cream of tartar

1 teaspoon table salt

2 teaspoons pure vanilla extract

4 tablespoons citrus fruit zest
(lemon, orange, or lime)

2 teaspoons fresh citrus juice
(lemon, orange, or lime)

Ginger-Tarragon Berries
(see recipe)

Vanilla Whipped Cream
(see recipe)

¼ cup raw sugar

1 lime, zested

Preheat oven to 350°F.

Sift flour with 6 ounces of the sugar, and set aside. Whisk egg whites, cream of tartar, salt, and vanilla until foamy. Slowly add remaining 6 ounces of the sugar to egg white mixture while whisking. Continue whisking until egg whites hold a ribbon but not peaks. Add one-third of the sifted flour, and fold into egg whites. Fold in another one-third of the sifted flour, and repeat with remaining one-third of the sifted flour. Fold in zest and juice.

Project Pastry: Desserts, Tailor Made

One of the pastry chefs at Hell's Kitchen is Katherine Gerdes, daughter of co-owner Cynthia Gerdes. A clothing designer by trade (she competed in the third season of *Project Runway*), Katy is also an accomplished baker. When Hell's Kitchen added dinner service, the demand for dessert soared, and Mitch and Steve turned to Katy. Since her design business allows her some flexibility, she was able to help them out. She lured another baker to hell, as well, and together they turn out some pretty heavenly creations.

For individual cakes, remove tops and bottoms of 8 (15-ounce) fruit cans, rinsed and with labels removed. Line a rimmed baking sheet with parchment paper, and place cans on the sheet. Divide batter into cans (see note), and bake on the center rack of the oven 30 to 45 minutes, or until tops are golden brown and spring back when touched.

Remove from the oven. Place a wire rack on top of the cans and flip. Let cakes cool in the cans at least 1 hour. Serve with ginger-tarragon berries and vanilla whipped cream. Mix raw sugar and lime zest, and sprinkle on top.

NOTE: Batter will also make enough for 1 regular-sized angel food (tube) pan.

GINGER-TARRAGON BERRIES

1 quart strawberries, quartered

½ pint blueberries

½ pint blackberries

⅓ cup granulated sugar

¼ cup minced fresh tarragon

2 tablespoons chopped candied ginger

Toss together all ingredients, and let rest 15 minutes. Makes about 4 cups.

VANILLA WHIPPED CREAM

2 cups heavy whipping cream

1 tablespoon pure vanilla extract

½ cup sugar

Add all ingredients to a cold stainless steel bowl, and whip until medium-stiff peaks form. Makes about 4 cups.

BRIOCHE BREAD PUDDING
WITH CRÈME ANGLAISE `MAKES ABOUT 2 CUPS`

7 thick slices Brioche Bread, cubed (4 cups) (see recipe, p. 203)

⅓ cup unsalted butter, melted

4 large eggs, beaten

2¼ cups whole milk

½ cup granulated sugar

1 tablespoon pure vanilla extract

½ teaspoon ground cinnamon

½ cup dried black currants

Crème Anglaise (see recipe)

Preheat oven to 300°F.

Place brioche cubes in a large bowl. Pour melted butter over cubes, and gently toss. Lay buttered cubes on a rimmed baking sheet in a single layer. Place on the center rack of the oven, and bake 15

minutes. Remove from the oven, and let cool to room temperature. Turn the oven's temperature up to 350°F.

Add eggs, milk, sugar, vanilla extract, and cinnamon to a large bowl, and whisk together well. Add brioche cubes and ¼ cup of the currants to another large bowl, and gently toss. Brush a 2-quart baking dish with melted butter, and fill with brioche mixture. Drizzle egg and milk mixture evenly over brioche, and sprinkle with remaining ¼ cup of the currants. Pat pudding down gently with a spatula.

Place baking dish on the center rack of the oven, and bake uncovered 41 to 47 minutes, or until a toothpick inserted into the center comes out clean. Remove dish from the oven, and let rest 11 minutes. Cut and plate pieces, and drizzle with crème anglaise. Serve immediately. Once cooled to room temperature, the bread pudding will keep for 3 days covered and refrigerated.

CRÈME ANGLAISE

1½ cups heavy cream

1½ cups whole milk

3 large egg yolks, well beaten

¼ cup granulated sugar

Vanilla bean

¼ teaspoon kosher salt

Place water in the bottom of a double boiler, and heat to a simmer over medium high. Place heavy cream and milk in the top of the double boiler. Cut vanilla bean in half lengthwise. Scrape pulp out of half of the pod, and finely chop half of the bean pod. Reserve other half of the vanilla bean for another use. Put both pulp and chopped pod into cream mixture. Heat cream mixture to a simmer, but do not let boil.

Place beaten egg yolks and sugar in a large bowl, and whisk together vigorously. Pour 1 cup of the warm cream mixture into yolk mixture, and whisk vigorously. Scrape egg mixture into simmering cream with a rubber spatula, and add salt. Whisk gently until sauce begins to thicken, 7 to 11 minutes. If sauce becomes too thick, thin with warm heavy cream.

Remove sauce from heat, strain through a fine mesh strainer, and discard solids. Serve warm, or let cool to room temperature and place in a container with a tight-fitting lid. Will keep refrigerated for no more than 3 days. Makes 4 cups.

COOKIE BRITTLE `MAKES UP TO 12 SERVINGS`

> Like the caramel roll recipe we use at the restaurants, this one was my dad's.
> He was a monster for sweets.

2 cups (4 sticks) unsalted butter,
at room temperature

1 cup granulated sugar

1 teaspoon kosher salt

2 teaspoons pure vanilla extract

3 cups all-purpose flour

1¼ cups chopped pecans

1¼ cups semisweet chocolate chunks

Preheat oven to 375°F.

Add butter and sugar to the bowl of a stand mixer, and cream until light and fluffy. Add salt and vanilla to creamed butter, and slowly add flour. Add pecans and chocolate, and mix until combined. Press dough into a greased rimmed baking sheet.

Place on the center rack of the oven, and bake 15 to 20 minutes, or until evenly browned. Remove from the oven, and let cool to room temperature. Flip the baking sheet onto a flat work surface, and break brittle into large chunks.

HELL'S KITCHEN PEANUT BUTTER CHOCOLATE CHIP COOKIES `MAKES 15 COOKIES`

1 cup (2 sticks) unsalted butter, at room temperature

1 cup firmly packed light brown sugar

1 cup granulated sugar

1½ cups Mitch's World-Famous Peanut Butter (see recipe, p. 143)

2 large eggs

1 teaspoon pure vanilla extract

1 teaspoon kosher salt

1 teaspoon baking soda

2 cups all-purpose flour

1 cup chocolate chips

Preheat oven to 325°F.

Add butter, brown sugar, and granulated sugar to the bowl of a stand mixer, and cream until pale and fluffy, scraping the sides and bottom of the bowl frequently. Add peanut butter, eggs, and vanilla, and continue to mix until blended. Whisk together salt, soda, and flour in a separate bowl. Slowly add flour mixture to peanut butter mixture, blending until just combined. Add chocolate chips, and mix until just combined.

Portion cookie dough into 15 large balls, and place balls, evenly spaced, onto a rimmed baking sheet lined with parchment paper. Press down lightly on the top of each ball. Place on the center rack of the oven, and bake 8 to 10 minutes, until golden brown. Remove from the oven, place cookies on a wire rack, and let cool.

HOT DAMN BUTTERED PRETZELS

4 teaspoons active dry yeast

½ cup + 1 teaspoon granulated sugar

1½ cups warm water, about 110°F

5 cups all-purpose flour

1½ teaspoons kosher salt

1 tablespoon vegetable oil

¼ cup baking soda

2 cups hot water

¼ cup fine sea salt

½ cup (1 stick) unsalted butter, melted

Preheat oven to 375°F.

Dissolve yeast and 1 teaspoon of the sugar in 1½ cups warm water in a small bowl. Whisk gently and let bloom, 3 to 5 minutes. Mix flour, ½ cup of the sugar, and salt in the bowl of a stand mixer fitted with a dough hook. Make a well in the center of the flour mixture, and add yeast mixture. Mix on low speed until well blended. If dough seems dry, add a few tablespoons warm water. Keep kneading until dough is smooth, about 7 to 8 minutes.

Lightly oil a large bowl, and place dough in it, turning to coat. Cover the bowl loosely with plastic wrap, and place in a warm area. Let rise until double in size, about 1 hour. Knead gently by hand 1 to 2 minutes. (You should not need any flour, and if you do, the dough is too wet. If too wet, add flour as needed.)

Divide into 8 equal pieces of about 5 ounces. Roll each piece into a short rope, about 8 inches long, and let rest 1 to 2 minutes. Roll each piece into a longer rope, about 25 to 30 inches, and twist into a pretzel shape. Cover pretzels loosely, and let rise, 10 to 15 minutes.

Dissolve baking soda in 2 cups hot water in a medium bowl. Dip each pretzel into baking soda solution, and place on a greased rimmed baking sheet. Sprinkle generously with sea salt. Place on the center rack of the oven, and bake 5 minutes. Rotate 180 degrees, and bake another 5 minutes, or until golden brown. Remove from the oven, and brush hot pretzels with melted butter. Pretzels are best served warm and are even better with Annie's Mustard (see recipe, p. 12).

Pretzels will keep at room temperature for 2 to 3 days (do not cover) or can be wrapped in plastic and frozen.

LIBATIONS: SPICY, COLD, AND HOT

BLOODY MARY MIX `MAKES ABOUT 6 CUPS`

5 cups Tomato Juice (see recipe)

⅓ cup fresh lemon juice

5 teaspoons lemon pepper

5 teaspoons celery salt

5 teaspoons Sweetened Ginger Purée (see recipe)

4 teaspoons Worcestershire sauce

3 teaspoons Tabasco sauce

2 teaspoons horseradish

Mix all ingredients in a large stainless steel, glass, or ceramic bowl. Place in a container with a tight-fitting lid. Will keep refrigerated for up to 1 week. Stir well before serving.

TOMATO JUICE

6 cups canned crushed tomatoes

2 cups bottled water

½ cup minced celery

½ cup minced white onion

1 tablespoon granulated sugar

1 large clove garlic, minced (2 teaspoons)

3 tablespoons liquor from a jar of Peppadew peppers (see note)

3 tablespoons fresh lemon juice

2 tablespoons Worcestershire sauce

1 teaspoon ground white pepper

½ teaspoon fresh horseradish

Heat tomato fillets, bottled water, minced celery, minced onion, sugar, and garlic to a boil in a large saucepan over medium high. Reduce heat to a simmer, stirring frequently, 25 to 31 minutes.

Place tomato mixture in a food processor fitted with a steel chopping blade or in a blender, and purée 17 to 21 seconds, or until mixture is smooth. Strain through a fine mesh sieve into the saucepan, and press on solids with a spoon or the back of a ladle to extract as much liquid as possible. This should yield about 5½ cups. Discard solids.

Add Peppadew pepper liquor, lemon juice, Worcestershire sauce, white pepper, and horseradish to the saucepan. Simmer over medium heat 11 minutes. Remove from heat, and let cool to room temperature.

Adjust seasoning, and place juice in a stainless steel, glass, or ceramic container with a tight-fitting lid. Will keep refrigerated for up to 1 week. Stir well before serving, and garnish with lemon wedges. Makes about 6 cups.

NOTE: We use these peppers in the salsa recipe on p. 146. This is one of the applications for the reserved liquor.

SWEETENED GINGER PURÉE

2 cups grated fresh ginger

1 cup granulated sugar

1 whole lemon, juiced

Heat all ingredients in a small saucepan over medium until nearly all moisture has evaporated. Remove from heat, and let cool to room temperature. Place in a food processor fitted with a steel chopping blade, and purée until smooth, 3 to 5 seconds. Put ginger purée in a stainless steel, glass, or ceramic container with a tight-fitting lid and refrigerate. Will keep refrigerated up to 1 month. Makes about 2 cups.

BEER MARGARITA   `MAKES 4 SERVINGS`

I particularly like this recipe because it becomes a margarita with a head on it. It really is beautiful.

¾ cup frozen limeade

¾ cup Summit Extra Pale Ale

¾ cup tequila

Fresh lime wedges

Place limeade, ale, and tequila in a blender and top with ice cubes. Blend the shit out of it, and pour mixture into 4 margarita glasses (or 1 small vase, in the case of me during my drinking days). Garnish with lime wedges.

HOT DAMN COCOA   `MAKES 1 SERVING`

2½ tablespoons Hot Damn Cocoa Mix
(see recipe)

1 cup whole milk

Homemade Miniature Marshmallows
(see recipe)

Heat milk in a small saucepan until just simmering; do not let milk boil. Whisk in cocoa mix, and stir vigorously. Pour into a mugh, and top with marshmallows and/or whipped cream (see recipe, p. 23), and dust lightly with more of the cocoa mix.

HOT DAMN COCOA MIX

2½ cups Vanilla Sugar (see recipe)

1⅓ cups unsweetened Dutch-process cocoa powder

2 teaspoons ground cinnamon

½ teaspoon kosher salt

⅛ teaspoon grated fresh nutmeg

Place all ingredients in a medium bowl, and mix together well. Store in a stainless steel, glass, or ceramic container with a tight-fitting lid. Will keep damn near indefinitely. Makes about 4 cups.

VANILLA SUGAR

1½ cups granulated sugar

⅓ cup firmly packed light brown sugar

⅓ cup powdered sugar

3 tablespoons vanilla powder
(see note)

1 whole vanilla bean

Place granulated sugar, brown sugar, powdered sugar, and vanilla powder in the bowl of a stand mixer fitted with a paddle. Blend on low speed until well mixed. Or whisk together in a large bowl. Split vanilla bean in half lengthwise, and scrape pulp into sugar mixture with a sharp knife. Mince bean pod with the knife, and add to sugar mixture. Blend on low speed until well incorporated, about 3 minutes. Place vanilla sugar in a stainless steel, glass, or ceramic container with a tight-fitting lid. Will keep indefinitely. To use, strain amount of vanilla sugar needed through a fine mesh sieve, and return chunks of the vanilla pod back into any saved sugar. Makes about 2¼ cups.

NOTE: Vanilla powder can be hard to locate, though it can be found at specialty food stores. If you can't find it, just omit it from the recipe.

HOMEMADE MINIATURE MARSHMALLOWS

Homemade marshmallows are far, far, far superior to their store-bought illegitimate cousins. They're creamier, fluffier, and more flavorful. If you've never tasted a homemade marshmallow and you're basing a like or dislike of marshmallows on those hard little pellets you buy in the grocery store, just STOP. Take the time to give these a try.

5 tablespoons + 1 teaspoon ice water

2 packets unflavored gelatin

5 tablespoons + 1 teaspoon water

2/3 cup light corn syrup

6 tablespoons granulated sugar

1/8 teaspoon kosher salt

1/2 teaspoon pure vanilla extract

3 tablespoons powdered sugar

3 tablespoons cornstarch

Gently mix 5 tablespoons + 1 teaspoon ice water and gelatin in a small bowl, and set aside.

Heat to a simmer 5 tablespoons + 1 teaspoon water, corn syrup, granulated sugar, and salt in a small, heavy saucepan over medium high. Cover the pan, and let simmer 3 to 5 minutes. Uncover and clip on a candy thermometer, with its bulb in the corn syrup mixture but *not* touching the bottom of the pan. Continue to simmer until the thermometer reads 250°F, about 7 to 9 minutes, and then remove the pan from heat immediately.

Pour corn syrup mixture into the bowl of a stand mixer fitted with a wire whip, and mix on medium speed, slowly pouring in gelatin mixture. Increase speed to high, and mix until very thick, about 13 to 15 minutes. With the mixer still running, add vanilla extract, and mix 1 minute more.

Combine powdered sugar and cornstarch in a small bowl. Line three rimmed baking sheets with parchment paper, and spray paper with nonstick cooking spray. Dust with 2 tablespoons of the powdered sugar mixture.

With a rubber spatula, spoon whisked corn syrup mixture into a pastry bag fitted with a ½-inch round pastry tip. Pipe mixture in long strips the length of the pans, about 1 inch apart. Dust tops of the strips with 2 more tablespoons of the powdered sugar mixture, and let rest 4 to 5 hours. Dust strips with the remaining powdered sugar mixture, and gently roll in excess powder. Let set uncovered at room temperature overnight.

The next day, cut strips into ½-inch pieces with a sharp knife. Roll marshmallows in excess powdered sugar mixture. Place marshmallows in a container with a tight-fitting lid, and store in a cool, dry place. Will keep up to 1 month. Makes about 1 pound.

CUISINE SAVAGE

Recipes for Wild Game and Quarry

"Be as I am—a reluctant enthusiast . . . a part-time crusader, a half-hearted fanatic. Save the other half for yourselves and your lives for pleasure and adventure. It is not enough to fight for the land; it is even more important to enjoy it. While you can. While it's still here. So get out there and hunt and fish and mess around with your friends, ramble out yonder and explore the forests, encounter the grizz, climb the mountains, bag the peaks, run the rivers, breathe deep of that yet sweet and lucid air, sit quietly for a while and contemplate the precious stillness, that lovely, mysterious and awesome space."

EDWARD ABBEY

There is a certain kind of chef who is also a wild gatherer, a huntsman, and a rabbi who both sacrifices and blesses the animals he kills. Mitch Omer is one of these.

Since his childhood in Iowa, Mitch has been an outdoorsman. In spring, when the weather turned warm and soft, he and his father would go morel hunting. And in fall, after the first couple frosts had crisped the farmland and woods around Des Moines, they would leave before dawn—shotguns over their shoulders—and trudge through fallen maple leaves turned russet and gold.

From a very early age Mitch knew how to gut and skin newly dead creatures: shaving the hide away from the meat, breaking the animal down following muscles and tendons, tying it and hanging it, moving on to hunt more. And when they returned home—no matter how far away home was—they would cook together: fried mushrooms, biscuits with rabbit gravy, roasted venison with root vegetables, pan-fried trout.

These days, Mitch can't steady a gun in his hands, and his love for fishing has waned since his father died. But he still loves and collects weapons: sniper rifles, pistols, buffalo guns, a variety of crossbows and knives. And he continues to go bear hunting each year because even with the shaking from his meds, a bear is a target he might be able to hit.

Morels

"I can't remember ever *not* morel hunting," Mitch says now.

Together, Mitch and his father tromped through clear, sun-dappled mornings, green leaves overhead, the air moist with spring wind. Often, Dana would stop and say, "Look around you," or simply, "Pay attention," and Mitch at eight or ten or fifteen would do as his dad said. They scouted for mounds of dead leaves that might be covering and feeding a cache of wild fungus underneath.

Finding morels means developing a nose for the spunky scent that tells you where they lie. Impatient in every other area of his life, Mitch developed a love for the quiet hard work of foraging. After a day out in the woods, he and Dana would haul a basket of the brainy little mushrooms home and clean, bread, and fry them, squeezing fresh lemon juice over the top before they ate.

In adulthood, no matter how wild or fractious the rest of his life, Mitch continued the annual rite of morel hunting, leading groups through the outskirts of the Twin Cities the way his father had once led him. In the late 1980s one of his culinary heroes—the chef Jacques Pépin—came to Minneapolis for a cooking demonstration. Mitch showed up there, elbowed his way to Pépin, and handed over a sack of fresh morels.

The next day, the two (along with Pépin's local hosts) went out morel hunting together and happened across a valley that was literally blanketed with them. They gathered until their hands were cramping and then took the haul back to the home of one of their group, and Pépin made omelets with morels, Gruyère, and just a hint of garlic.

Morel Omelet à la Jacques Pépin

2 tablespoons unsalted butter, divided

⅓ cup coarsely chopped fresh or reconstituted morels

1 teaspoon minced shallot

1 small clove garlic, minced (½ teaspoon)

¼ cup shredded Gruyère (1 ounce)

2 extra-large eggs

2 tablespoons heavy cream

Kosher salt

Ground black pepper

Jacques's guide, Mitch, with a fifty-pound morel haul

Melt 1 tablespoon of the butter in a medium skillet over medium-high heat, until bubbling. Add chopped morels, and stir to mix well with butter. Add shallots and garlic. Turn heat to high, and cook, stirring continually, for 13 seconds. Remove from heat. Crack eggs into a small bowl, and add heavy cream. Beat vigorously with a fork.

Heat remaining 1 tablespoon of the butter in an 8-inch nonstick skillet over medium high. Add egg mixture, and stir vigorously with a rubber spatula, about 9 seconds. Stop stirring, and reduce heat to medium. Allow eggs to cook another 15 to 21 seconds undisturbed. Flip eggs over. Spoon morel mixture onto the center, and sprinkle with cheese.

Remove the pan from heat, and fold an edge of the omelet about one-third of the way to the center. Fold the opposite edge toward the center. Slide omelet onto a plate and serve. Makes 1 omelet.

Fried Morels

1 cup whole milk

3 large eggs

2 cups all-purpose flour

2 tablespoons lemon pepper

1 pound fresh morels, cleaned

2 cups (4 sticks) unsalted butter

Kosher salt

Fresh lemon wedges

Whisk together milk and eggs in a medium bowl, and set aside. Place flour in another bowl, and mix in lemon pepper. Dip morels in egg wash, and then dredge in flour mixture.

Melt 1 cup of the butter in a large, heavy skillet over medium-high heat, until bubbling. Add half of the breaded morels. Fry undisturbed about 3 to 5 minutes, until bottoms are golden brown. Flip morels, and continue frying 1 to 3 minutes more.

Remove fried morels from the pan with a slotted spoon, and drain on a double thickness of paper towels. Season with kosher salt, and squeeze lemon juice over. Wipe out the pan before frying the second batch and then repeat. Serve hot.

Ancient Romans referred to mushrooms as the food of the gods, and eating fried morels has brought me as close as I've been to agreeing with them. If there's any one great food, it's morels. This is how we always ate them when I was younger. Two or three families would gather at the house around a kitchen table, breading and frying and eating piles of fried morels in a wine-lubricated evening of gluttony.

Mushroom-Crusted Shrimp Quiche

4 tablespoons (½ stick) unsalted butter

¾ cup coarsely chopped leek (about ½ medium leek, white part only), rinsed under cold running water

½ pound shrimp (U-15s), peeled, deveined, and coarsely chopped

1 Quiche Shell with Morels (see recipe)

4¼ cups shredded Gruyère (17 ounces)

1 cup large-curd cottage cheese, at room temperature

3 extra-large eggs

1 cup heavy cream

½ teaspoon garlic salt

¼ teaspoon cayenne

1 teaspoon ground black pepper

Preheat oven to 350°F.

Melt butter in a large skillet over medium-high heat. Add leeks, and cook, stirring continually, 1 to 3 minutes. Add shrimp, and cook and stir until just warmed through, about 1 minute.

Scrape leeks and shrimp into quiche shell with a rubber spatula, and spread evenly over the bottom. Sprinkle Gruyère evenly over shrimp mixture, and spread cottage cheese evenly over Gruyère.

Place eggs, cream, salt, cayenne, and black pepper in a food processor fitted with a steel chop-

ping blade, and purée until smooth, 5 to 7 seconds. Pour egg mixture over leeks, shrimp, and cheese. Place the pie pan on the center rack of the oven, and bake 25 to 30 minutes, or until a knife inserted into the center comes out clean. Let rest 11 to 17 minutes before cutting. Makes 6 servings.

QUICHE SHELL WITH MORELS

3 tablespoons unsalted butter

2 medium cloves garlic, minced (2 teaspoons)

10 ounces fresh morels, cleaned and finely chopped

½ cup crushed saltine crackers

Melt butter in a large skillet over medium-high heat. Add minced garlic, and stir vigorously 1 to 3 minutes, until garlic begins to brown. Stir in chopped morels, and cook 5 to 7 minutes, stirring continually. Remove the skillet from heat. Add crushed cracker crumbs, and stir to mix well. Butter a 9-inch pie pan, and press cracker mixture evenly into the bottom and sides. Place shell in the refrigerator for at least 2 hours to set. Makes 1 shell.

Rabbit

They never really meant to go rabbit hunting. Typically, Mitch and his father would be out shooting pheasants, and they'd run across a patch where rabbits were plentiful, skittering across the open copse like frantic actors on a stage. They were fast and small—hard to hit—which made the sport of hunting them more challenging and in some ways more fun.

Mitch quit rabbit hunting after a while because it was difficult to kill the animals with a single shot, and finishing them off usually involved breaking their necks. He didn't have the stomach for it. But Dana, who loved rabbit meat, did, leaping up to grab the long ears and twisting the furry little head, putting the bunny out of its misery with dispatch.

Rabbit is purported by many fans to taste like chicken. But that's inaccurate, Mitch says. It is a light, white meat, but it has a hint of gamey flavor—just a little dark wildness—in the flavor palate below.

Biscuits with Rabbit Gravy

4 tablespoons (½ stick) unsalted butter

½ pound coarsely chopped rabbit meat

2 tablespoons all-purpose flour

1 cup chicken stock

2 cups heavy cream

8 Biscuits (recipe below)

Heat butter in a medium saucepan over medium high. Add chopped rabbit meat, and cook, stirring continually, until heated through, about 3 minutes. Add flour, and stir vigorously until

rabbit is evenly coated. Stir in chicken stock, and whisk until gravy begins to thicken. Add heavy cream, and whisking continually, heat gravy just to a boil. Remove immediately from heat, and season with salt and pepper. Place 2 warm biscuits on each of 4 plates, and ladle gravy over biscuits. Makes 4 servings.

BISCUITS

2 cups all-purpose flour

1½ teaspoons baking powder

½ teaspoon baking soda

½ teaspoon kosher salt

11 tablespoons cold butter, cut into small pieces

¾ cup cold buttermilk

½ cup (1 stick) unsalted butter, melted

Preheat oven to 500°F.

Place flour, baking powder, soda, and salt in the bowl of a stand mixer fitted with a paddle, and mix together on medium speed. Add cold butter, and blend until you reach a coarse meal consistency. Slowly add buttermilk, but do not allow dough to ball up.

Turn dough onto a floured surface, and knead gently to distribute moisture evenly and make dough less sticky. Gently roll out to a ½-inch thickness. Dip a 3-inch biscuit cutter into flour, and press into dough. Do *not* twist cutter; this distorts the sides of biscuits. Place cut-out biscuits on a rimmed baking sheet lined with parchment paper. Press any scraps of the remaining dough together, and roll out again to a ½-inch thickness. Cut more biscuits. Discard any scraps after cutting out second batch of biscuits.

Place on the center rack of the oven, and bake 11 to 15 minutes, until biscuits are well risen and slightly golden brown. Remove from the oven, and brush biscuits generously with melted butter. Makes 8 biscuits.

Chocolate Bunnies

The New French Café was one of the most innovative restaurants in the Twin Cities when I worked there in the 1980s, and that's where I came up with this recipe. I remember one evening while I was on the line making chocolate bunnies, I hit a lull and stepped out back to smoke a joint, but when I came back in, the restaurant was packed, and I was sorely behind. I never did regain my timing, which was an injustice given what patrons were paying for their meals. I have never gotten high at work again.

8 rabbit tenderloins

3 cups white zinfandel

4 oranges, juiced

2 medium cloves garlic, minced (2 teaspoons)

2 tablespoons minced carrot

2 tablespoons minced white onion

2 tablespoons minced celery

1 large sprig fresh rosemary

2 large sprigs fresh thyme

4 tablespoons (½ stick) unsalted butter

1 cup rich veal stock

4 tablespoons (½ stick) cold butter, cut into small pieces

2 ounces unsweetened chocolate, chopped fine

Olive oil

Kosher salt

Ground black pepper

In an air-tight stainless steel, glass, or ceramic container, place rabbit tenderloins in a marinade made of wine, orange juice, garlic, carrot, onion, celery, rosemary, and thyme, and refrigerate 2 to 3 hours.

Prepare an outdoor grill with hot coals, and set a grill rack 4 inches from the coals (set heat to high if using a gas grill).

Remove tenderloins from marinade, and set aside. Remove rosemary and thyme from marinade and discard. Strain marinade through a fine mesh sieve into a bowl, and set aside, reserving garlic, carrot, onion, and celery.

Melt butter in a large skillet over medium-high heat. Add reserved garlic, carrot, onion, and celery. Turn heat to high, and stirring continually, brown vegetables. Add reserved marinade, and reduce by half. Add veal stock, and reduce by half again. Remove the skillet from heat, and strain sauce into a bowl, discarding solids. Return sauce to the skillet, and heat to a boil. Remove from heat, and whisk in cold butter. When butter emulsifies, whisk in chocolate.

Brush tenderloins with olive oil, and sprinkle lightly with salt and pepper. Grill directly over hot coals, about 3 minutes per side. Remove from heat, and let rest 5 minutes.

To serve, nap each plate with sauce, and top with 2 tenderloins, cut on a bias and fanned out over sauce. Makes 4 servings.

Trout

They were on their last official father-son hunting trip, in Wyoming, the summer before Mitch went to Iowa State, when Dana spotted a crystal-clear brook packed with trout. He dropped his gun, kicked off his shoes, rolled up his pants, and splashed in. The fish scattered, but Dana slid his hands under rocks and scooped the trout up, throwing them to Mitch up on the bank, shouting at him to kill them by bashing their heads with a rock.

This was, apparently, the way Dana typically fished for trout: bear-like. Spooking the fish, watching where they went, and scooping them out by hand. When they went back to camp that night—with a deer as well as a string of fish—they fried up the trout with burnt butter and eggs.

Fancy Fried Trout with Scrambled Eggs and Burnt Butter

4 sides brook trout, skinned and filleted

1 cup buttermilk

1 cup panko bread crumbs (see note, p. 42)

1 cup coarse-ground cornmeal (polenta)

3 tablespoons lemon pepper

1¾ cups (3½ sticks) unsalted butter, divided

½ lemon, juiced

4 large eggs

6 tablespoons heavy cream

Kosher salt

Ground black pepper

Place trout fillets in a glass or ceramic dish, and cover with buttermilk. Cover the dish with plastic wrap, and refrigerate at least 2 hours. Remove fillets from buttermilk, and discard liquid. Mix bread crumbs, cornmeal, and lemon pepper in a large bowl. Dredge fillets through bread crumb mixture, and set aside.

Melt ½ cup (1 stick) of the butter in a large skillet over medium-high heat, until bubbling. Add breaded trout, and cook undisturbed until bread crumbs only begin to brown, about 3 minutes each side. Remove fillets, and hold in warm oven.

Heat ¾ cup (2½ sticks) of the butter in the same skillet until it just begins to smoke. Remove the skillet from heat, add lemon juice, and set aside.

Melt remaining ½ cup (1 stick) butter in a medium skillet. Crack eggs into the skillet, and whisk to break yolks. Add heavy cream, and stir with a rubber spatula until eggs come together. Remove from heat, and season with salt and pepper.

To serve, place 1 fried trout fillet on each plate. Divide eggs, placing one-quarter of the eggs on top of each trout fillet, and then drizzle with burnt-butter sauce. Makes 4 servings.

Venison

Mitch shot his first deer on that same trip to Wyoming. Or rather, he held the gun while his father shot . . .

Hunting licenses were tough to come by, and they had only one between the two of them, so the deal they made was that Dana would look for deer but only Mitch would shoot. After hours of hiking, they came to a clearing. Mitch saw nothing. Suddenly, his father grabbed the rifle that lay over his shoulder and hissed at Mitch to hold still. The next second, the gun went off and dropped a buck that had been sprinting across the hillside. To this day, Mitch has tinnitus in his left ear from that single shot.

As a chef he's cooked plenty of venison—which means not only deer but elk, caribou, and moose. Any antlered creature of the genus *Cervidae* qualifies. You can make the following with whatever venison you happen to have on hand.

Roasted Venison with Root Vegetables over Soft Polenta

1 whole venison tenderloin, about 3 pounds

4 tablespoons extra-virgin olive oil

4 tablespoons sea salt

½ cup (1 stick) unsalted butter

8 whole medium cloves garlic

1 cup pearl onions

1 cup coarsely chopped carrots

1 cup coarsely chopped turnips

2 cups rich veal stock

2 tablespoons granulated sugar

4 cups Soft Polenta (see recipe)

If there is one lesson I have to teach in this area, it is to never overcook game! A lot of cooks have the mistaken notion that game has to be cooked forever. In many such instances clean, fresh flavors are lost almost entirely. In order to retain its natural juices, a tenderloin of venison should never be cooked beyond medium rare.

Preheat oven to 375°F.

Trim tenderloin of any silver skin (the connective tissue between the tenderloin muscle and its surface fat). Rub with olive oil, and season with salt. Place on a rimmed baking sheet, and put on the center rack of the oven. Check with a meat thermometer after 15 minutes and about every 19 minutes after that. Remove from the oven when the interior temperature reads 110°F. (No higher!) Let rest at least 15 minutes.

Prepare polenta while meat is cooking.

Melt butter in a large saucepan over medium-high heat until it just begins to smoke. Add garlic, onions, carrots, and turnips, and cook, stirring continually, until browned, about 7 minutes. Add veal stock and sugar, and stir to mix well. Reduce heat to a simmer. Cover the pan, and cook until most of the liquid has been absorbed, about 10 minutes. Remove from heat, but leave covered.

To serve, spoon polenta onto each plate. Slice tenderloin into 12 thick medallions. Arrange 3 slices of venison over each mound of polenta. Spoon vegetables and broth over top. Makes 4 servings.

SOFT POLENTA

6 cups rich chicken broth

2 tablespoons olive oil

2 tablespoons unsalted butter

1 teaspoon kosher salt

1½ cups polenta (coarse-ground cornmeal)

¾ cup grated Parmesan cheese

Ground black pepper

Heat chicken broth to a boil in a large, heavy saucepan. Add olive oil, butter, and salt, and reduce heat to low. Gradually whisk in polenta, and stir continually 15 to 21 minutes, or until mixture is smooth. Stir in Parmesan, and season with pepper. Remove from heat, and cover to keep warm. Makes 6½ cups.

Antelope

Antelope—which is different from venison—is unlike any other quarry. They are skittish animals and lightning fast, so rather than tracking them like deer, it's necessary to sight antelope

from a great distance and shoot with dead aim. Mitch admits he simply doesn't have the skill; he didn't even before he lost what acuteness he had to psychotropic drugs. But Pappy was a marksman—the sort of guy for whom a rifle was an extension of his eyes and arms—who once scored a double. He didn't even mean to. He'd actually *seen* only one antelope, and he felled it on the spot. When Pappy went to retrieve his kill, he found a second dead antelope behind the first. His bullet had passed through them both. Mitch was so awed he created this recipe.

Antelope Stroganoff

½ cup (1 stick) unsalted butter

3 pounds boneless antelope leg or shoulder, cut into 4-inch cubes

6 whole medium cloves garlic

½ pound pearl onions, peeled

½ pound whole crimini mushrooms

½ cup all-purpose flour

1 tablespoon kosher salt

1 tablespoon ground black pepper

1 cup rich beef broth

1½ cups sour cream

1 pound Egg Noodles (see recipe, p. 18)

½ cup (1 stick) unsalted butter, cut up

4 tablespoons minced fresh parsley

Prepare but do not cook Egg Noodles.

Melt ½ cup butter in a large, heavy Dutch oven over medium-high heat. Add antelope meat, and turn heat to high. Cook, stirring continually, until meat browns, about 7 minutes. Remove meat to a plate.

Return the Dutch oven to medium-high heat, and add garlic, onions, and mushrooms. Cook, stirring continually, for 3 to 4 minutes. Mix flour, salt, and pepper in a small bowl. Sprinkle in seasoned flour, and stir to mix well. Add beef broth, and whisk vigorously. Slowly bring broth mixture to a boil, whisking continually. Reduce heat to a simmer, and add sour cream. Whisk again and reduce heat. Add sautéed meat, and simmer 11 to 17 minutes.

Heat 3 quarts of water and 2 tablespoons kosher salt to a boil in a large pot for the noodles. Drop egg noodles in boiling water, and cook 7 to 9 minutes. Drain noodles in a colander, place in a large bowl, and toss with ½ cup cut-up butter. Add minced parsley, and toss well to evenly distribute.

Divide egg noodles among 4 plates, and ladle antelope stroganoff over. Makes 4 servings.

Bear

For Mitch and Pappy, bear hunting was a sacred ritual. Their hunting ground was on the edge of the White Earth Band of Ojibwe's reservation in northern Minnesota, and their guide, Bruce, was a great friend, as well as a member of the tribe.

It's hunting that requires enormous amounts of preparation. Each day, you have to bait the pits with approximately five gallons of fryer grease, a case of marshmallows, a dozen ears of corn, a quart of honey, and a rack of bacon. This is expensive, messy, back-breaking work. And then you wait, on mostly frigid autumn nights under the Northern Lights. You might be there all night, but it's important to stay alert. An approaching bear will make less noise than a chipmunk, Mitch says with awe. In order to bag one, you often sit in a pit for hours, motionless, simply absorbing the dark and the cold, the smell of wind. When the bear finally arrives, it's a shock and a gift.

Bruce's Rib Roast of Bear

Bear meat is unbelievably sweet and tender, roughly comparable to a supremely good grade of beef.

½ cup extra-virgin olive oil

¼ cup dry white wine

3 medium cloves garlic, minced (1 tablespoon)

3 tablespoons Dijon mustard

3 tablespoons minced crimini mushrooms

3 tablespoons minced white onion

2 tablespoons soy sauce

2 tablespoons unsalted butter, melted

½ teaspoon celery salt

½ teaspoon ground black pepper

1 (3- to 4½-pound) rib roast of bear

Mix olive oil, wine, garlic, mustard, mushrooms, onion, soy sauce, butter, celery salt, and black pepper in a large bowl. Place rib roast in a glass or ceramic dish, and cover with marinade. Cover dish with plastic wrap, and refrigerate 6 to 7 hours, turning every 2 to 3 hours to coat evenly.

Preheat oven to 375°F.

Remove roast from marinade, and place on a rimmed baking sheet, reserving marinade. Place on the center rack of the oven, and roast, checking with a meat thermometer after 15 minutes.

Meanwhile, heat marinade to a boil in a medium saucepan over medium, and boil 3 minutes. Baste roast with boiled marinade every 7 to 9 minutes.

Remove roast from the oven when a meat thermometer registers an internal temperature of 150°F, about 1 to 1½ hours. Let rest 15 to 21 minutes before serving. Makes 4 servings.

Walleye

A purist at heart, Mitch likes the *idea* of trudging out to the middle of a frozen lake, dressed like an Inupiat and sitting on a pickle bucket where the temperature—with wind chill—is 20 below. But in days past the hedonist in him won out. When he went ice fishing for walleye, it was in an igloo outfitted with plenty of wine, a propane heater, and a bench for two.

While fishing from just such an igloo with his friends, Mitch got uncomfortably warm in the full-force heat coming from the little propane device. As the temperature in the hut rose, he began to shed his clothes. By the time the walleye started to bite, he was three sheets to the wind and buck naked. This is, he says looking back, undoubtedly the very best way to ice fish.

Ice fishing *au naturel*

Extra-Fancy Walleye BLT

OK, so this sandwich isn't a whole lot different from the walleye BLT we make at Hell's Kitchen (see recipe, p. 104). But it uses more bacon, Crisco instead of lard, and a different tartar sauce. Also, this is my cookbook, so I can do whatever I damn well want.

4 (4- to 6-ounce) walleye fillets, skinned

2½ cups whole milk, divided

12 slices Nueske's thick-sliced applewood-smoked bacon

2 cups all-purpose flour

¾ cup cornstarch, divided

¼ cup lemon pepper

6 extra-large eggs

2 cups panko bread crumbs (see note, p. 42)

2 cups grated Parmesan cheese (6 ounces)

Crisco shortening (4 to 5 cups)

8 slices sourdough bread

½ cup (1 stick) unsalted butter

12 leaves butter lettuce

8 thick slices vine-ripened tomato

1 cup Scallion-Jalapeño Tartar Sauce (see recipe)

Place walleye fillets in a large baking dish in a single layer, and cover with 1 cup of the milk.

Refrigerate at least 1 hour.

Preheat oven to 375°F.

Prepare Scallion-Jalapeño Tartar Sauce and refrigerate.

Lay out bacon in a single layer on a rimmed baking sheet, and place on the center rack of the oven. Bake 21 to 25 minutes. Remove from the oven, and drain off grease and reserve. Turn bacon over, and return to the oven. Bake another 11 to 15 minutes, depending on how crisp you like your bacon. Remove from the oven, and let rest in the pan 5 minutes. Drain and reserve grease. Place bacon on a double thickness of paper towels, and blot excess grease with more paper towels. Set aside.

Mix flour, ½ cup of the cornstarch, and lemon pepper in a large bowl. Crack eggs into another large bowl, and whisk vigorously; add remaining 1½ cups of the milk, and whisk again to incorporate well. Add bread crumbs, Parmesan, and remaining ¼ cup of the cornstarch to a third bowl, and mix well.

Remove fish from the refrigerator, and take out of the pan, allowing excess milk to drip off. Dredge each fillet in seasoned flour, and press well to adhere flour to the flesh of the fish. Dip floured fillets in egg wash, and allow excess liquid to drain. Dredge in bread crumb mixture, gently pressing in breading.

Melt enough shortening in a large, deep-sided cast iron skillet to create about 2 inches of liquid fat. When melted shortening just begins to smoke, at about 375°F, add breaded fillets. Cook until breading turns a light brown, about 3 minutes. Turn fillets over, and cook another 1 to 3 minutes. Remove with a slotted spatula, and drain on a double thickness of paper towel. (See "Mitch's Primer on Deep-Frying," p. 103.)

Toast bread slices (or fry in reserved bacon grease), and butter 1 side of each slice with about 1 tablespoon of the butter. Lay toast on a work surface, and spread tartar sauce evenly on buttered side of each piece. Place 3 leaves of the butter lettuce on 4 pieces of the toast, and arrange 2 slices of the tomatoes on each pile of lettuce leaves. Place 1 deep-fried fillet on each set of the tomatoes, and lay 4 slices of the bacon on top of each fillet. Cover each sandwich with 1 of the remaining pieces of toast. Press sandwiches down slightly. Cut on a strong bias, and serve. Makes 4 sandwiches.

SCALLION-JALAPEÑO TARTAR SAUCE

¾ cup Miracle Whip

1¼ cups minced scallions, both white and green parts

¼ cup fresh lemon juice

2 fresh jalapeños, seeded and minced

1 large head garlic, minced (3 tablespoons)

1 tablespoon lemon pepper

Whisk together all ingredients in a large stainless steel, glass, or ceramic bowl. Cover and refrigerate. Makes about 4¼ cups.

Salmon

His first experience trawling for salmon was not ideal.

Mitch was living in California circa 1987 when friends asked if he'd like to go out deep-sea fishing. He'd worked all night, but thought what the hell. Before leaving, he dropped three tabs of acid, thinking it would mellow him out and help him enjoy the beauty of the San Francisco Bay. Instead, he had a bad trip . . . in every way. The day was rainy and cold and gray; Mitch was seasick, having pitching visions in psychedelic orange and green. Worse, the only thing he caught was a six-foot shark.

The last fishing trip

But decades later, he turned that karma around. Shortly before his father died, Mitch took Dana to Port Washington, Wisconsin, on a salmon fishing expedition for Father's Day. Weakened by congestive heart failure, Dana struggled to pull a single twenty-pound fish into the boat. But it was one of the happiest days father and son ever spent together. For the rest of the afternoon, Mitch worked both lines—his own and his dad's—while Dana sat back in the golden sunlight to watch.

Charred Salmon with Pineapple-Jalapeño Salsa

Remember, there is nothing better than properly cooked salmon and nothing worse than overcooked salmon. And for this recipe the fish absolutely must be cooked over an open flame, whether it's wood, charcoal, or gas. You cannot achieve perfection any other way.

4 (6-ounce) wild king or Coho salmon fillets

¼ cup + 3 tablespoons extra-virgin olive oil, divided

⅓ cup Dry Jamaican Jerk Seasoning (see recipe, p. 149)

¾ cup finely chopped golden pineapple

⅓ cup finely chopped red onion

1 fresh jalapeño, seeded and minced

3 teaspoons ground black pepper

1 teaspoon crushed red pepper

1 teaspoon kosher salt

Lemon Rice Pilaf (see recipe)

Brush tops of salmon fillets with 3 tablespoons of the olive oil. Sprinkle jerk seasoning liberally over fillets, pressing it firmly into the flesh. Refrigerate uncovered 2 hours or more.

To make salsa, add pineapple, red onion, jalapeño, black pepper, red pepper, salt, and ¼ cup of the olive oil to a small bowl, and mix well. Cover and refrigerate.

Remove salmon from the refrigerator ½ hour before cooking.

Prepare Lemon Rice Pilaf, and set aside.

Prepare an outdoor grill with hot coals, and set a grill rack 4 inches from the coals (set heat to high if using a gas grill).

Grill seasoned side of fillets until dark brown to light black, about 9 to 11 minutes. Turn over, and cook until just done, about 5 minutes. Do not overcook! The fish should be just warmed in the center, the steak equivalent of medium rare.

Plate with a side of the lemon rice pilaf, and top salmon with pineapple-jalapeño salsa. Makes 4 servings.

LEMON RICE PILAF

1½ cups rich chicken broth

¾ cup long grain rice

1 lemon, zested and juiced

3 tablespoons unsalted butter

2 teaspoons ground black pepper

2 teaspoons kosher salt

1 small white onion, finely chopped (½ cup)

¼ cup finely chopped celery

3 tablespoons minced red bell pepper

2 tablespoons minced fresh chives

Heat chicken broth in a medium saucepan until it just begins to simmer. Add rice, lemon zest, butter, black pepper, and salt, and stir to mix well. Heat to a boil, and then reduce heat. Cover and simmer about 15 minutes, or until rice is tender and liquid has been absorbed. Remove from heat. Add lemon juice, onion, celery, red pepper, and chives. Stir to mix well. Let rest 7 to 9 minutes. Stir well before serving. Makes about 2½ cups.

Salmon Elise

I developed this recipe for my eldest daughter, Jesse Elise. The only food she was interested in eating at the time were Happy Meals. Her favorite color was pink, so I made her a dish that would satisfy her culinary shortcomings.

4 (5-ounce) wild king or Coho salmon fillets

4 ounces fresh sea scallops

2 tablespoons lemon pepper

3 tablespoons peanut oil

1 (750 ml) bottle white zinfandel

3 shallots, minced

3 parsley sprigs

3 thyme sprigs

3 black peppercorns

1 bay leaf

½ cup (1 stick) cold unsalted butter, cut into small pieces

Beet Purée (see recipe)

Fresh lemon thyme leaves

Fresh mint leaves

Preheat oven to 375°F.

Cut salmon fillets in half lengthwise, and remove tops. Slice scallops into thin medallions, and layer on fillet bottoms. Cover with tops, and season with lemon pepper.

Heat peanut oil in a large ovenproof skillet over medium high, until just smoking. Add salmon fillets seasoned side down, and cook no more than 30 seconds. Carefully flip fillets, and cook another 30 seconds. Place the skillet in the oven, and bake approximately 9 to 11 minutes.

Bring wine, shallots, parsley, thyme, peppercorns, and bay leaf to a boil in a small saucepan over high heat. Continue boiling until volume is reduced by half. Remove from the heat. Strain liquid into a bowl, and discard solids. Heat wine mixture to a boil in a large skillet over high, and reduce again by half. Remove from the heat, and add cold butter, whisking vigorously until butter has emulsified.

To serve, spread sauce on each plate, and place a salmon fillet in the middle of each sauced plate. Place 3 mint leaves evenly around each fillet, and drop a dollop of beet purée on top of each mint leaf. Garnish fillets with fresh lemon thyme leaves. Makes 4 servings.

BEET PURÉE

1¼ pounds fresh beets, peeled and coarsely chopped

2 cups rich chicken broth

¼ cup (½ stick) unsalted butter

½ teaspoon ground cinnamon

Kosher salt

Ground black pepper

Place beets and chicken broth in a medium saucepan over medium high, and heat to a boil. Reduce heat, and simmer until beets are tender, 9 to 13 minutes. Remove from heat, strain, and discard liquid. Place beets in a food processor fitted with a steel chopping blade, and process about 5 seconds. Add butter and cinnamon, and process another 5 seconds. Scrape down the sides of the food processor with a rubber spatula, and season with salt and pepper. Process again until smooth, about 3 to 5 seconds. Will keep refrigerated 5 days. Makes about 4 cups.

SACRED RITES

Recipes for Funerals,
Weddings, and New Year's Day

Nearly every addict substitutes something for his addiction. Many smoke or suck on hard candy, trading one bad habit for another one on the theory that nicotine is better than heroin or tooth decay is preferable to liver disease. In the absence of alcohol, cocaine, meth, PCP, LSD, and tubs of fried chicken, Mitch puffs on a pipe constantly throughout the day. But his real substitute, the thing that keeps him upright, is ritual.

This isn't unusual either. What is AA but a new habit, one with predictable rhythms and comforts? It works for a lot of people but not for Mitch. His incantations have nothing to do with powerlessness or "turning himself over"; that's just not his style. Instead, he builds celebration and ceremony into everyday life: weddings, funerals, holidays. And it doesn't matter which one. Mitch throws himself equally into Halloween, the Fourth of July, and Elvis's birthday, which he marks at Hell's Kitchen with free peanut butter and banana sandwiches and bottles of red wine.

Christmas is a food, retail, glitter-spangled free-for-all. It starts in mid-December and lasts until well after New Year's. One tradition Mitch

Santa Mitch's elves

197

insists upon is the family tree viewing and progressive dinner—which takes nearly eight hours—where they travel from house to house, competing to see whose decorations are most lavish and whose food is best. Every year, Mitch claims to have won in both categories.

But no matter what the time of year, their life together—Mitch, Cynthia, their five combined children and one grandchild—is a perpetual series of events. If they go a week without a party or celebration of one kind or another, Mitch gets itchy. He buys gifts for no reason or finds a rationale for dressing up in drag. Once, when they were meeting his parents at Cosmos, one of Minneapolis's top restaurants, for their fifty-fifth wedding anniversary, Mitch insisted he and Cynthia go as trailer trash, in fake fur coats and rhinestone-studded glasses. He rented a limousine and spent the entire evening tipping everyone from the doorman to the busboy to the chef himself a dollar, which he flicked off a thick roll of ones.

Anything to turn an ordinary evening into a show.

Granted, he's been doing this since before he got sober. Everything from morel hunting to Sunday brunch has to become a kind of ceremony for Mitch. He loves fireworks and costumes and extravagant gifts. He loves presiding. So in 1978, when he spotted an ad in the back of *Rolling Stone* promising a real ordained minister's license from the Church of Mother Earth in return for a nominal fee, he tore it out on the spot and sent his money in.

It was a lark, only a novelty. At first. But once he started talking about his new "title," Mitch discovered people actually needed his services. Few of his friends were affiliated with churches, and they floundered when it came time to find a clergyperson for sacred rites. Who better to preside over life's critical events—marriage, baptism, death—than this mammoth man who'd studied every world religion and rejected them all yet found ecstasy in the everyday?

The requests (including mine . . . but that comes later) poured in. He's married everyone from a server and a busboy from the restaurant to the sister of a colleague who wanted a two-minute ceremony and requested that he stop by her table during lunch to say only, "By the power vested in me."

In one of the oddest twists on Mitch's story—and I realize that's saying a lot—he performed a wedding for his close friend Chris Bandy, the third in the triumvirate from Ely that includes Mitch and Pappy. Years later, Chris would divorce the woman he married that day under Reverend Omer and begin dating Mitch's own daughter, Jesse, who was twenty-five and literally half his age. Mitch and Cyn's only grandchild, a baby girl named Willow, is the product of that relationship. Chris has gone from beer-drinking, ice-fishing compatriot to common-law son-in-law. Assuming he does right by Jesse and the baby, Mitch has decided to let him live.

Though he continues to perform weddings, Mitch has gotten selective. He only takes on the couples he really wants to marry, and then he demands they prove their intentions by meeting with him at least twice and coming up with a meaningful plan that includes words, vows,

The Woman Behind, Beside, Under, and On Top of the Man

Mitch Omer's story is undeniably triumphant. Here's a man who's fought mental illness, addiction, poverty, obesity, and depression to come out a ragingly successful entrepreneur. But there's not a person in or around Hell's Kitchen who doesn't know the truth: Mitch and his brilliance are only the immediately visible part of the equation.

Behind the scenes—coming in at between 20 and 80 percent (depending upon the day)—is his wife and soul mate, Cyn.

He knows a good woman when he sees one

Until this woman, no one, including his parents, siblings, friends, bosses, and first two wives, really *got* Mitch. But Cynthia understands him better than he understands himself. She anticipates his moods, steers him away from self-destructive habits, controls his spending, and helps him organize all his random talents and thoughts. Without her he'd likely be a hapless, addled genius, the kind of troubled, high-potential guy people sigh about and say, "What a shame." It's mostly due to Cyn's constant care and attention that he's been able to turn his mania into an enormous asset. But make no mistake: this comes at a cost.

"Everyone else only gets that crazy, fun slice of Mitch," she says. "But I get the whole pie. And I feel it's my responsibility to be honest about what it's like to live with a bipolar addict. Sometimes, to be honest, it's hell."

When he's in a manic phase, Cyn talks about Mitch "getting on his high horse." He's invulnerable, impetuous, and commands all the attention in the room. Holidays are a dangerous time; like a child, he'll decide he wants . . . no *deserves* . . . everything he sees around Christmas. A new kayak, a bear gun, a digital camera, a set of Japanese knives. He'll leave all the party prep and busy work to her—Cyn buys all the gifts (including for his family) in addition to cleaning, doing laundry, entertaining at home, and making sure the Hell's Kitchen payroll shores up—and then take center stage and preside over every occasion like a satisfied king. He rarely sleeps, reads voraciously, compiles enormous lists, starts huge projects he never finishes, and outspends his paycheck by 200 percent. Like a magpie, he's attracted to shiny things.

But when Mitch is low, things are even worse. He's in dangerous territory, always on the brink of using again. Less than a month back from rehab, he had rotator cuff surgery and got hooked on the Vicocin his doctor prescribed for pain. He asked his employees to supply him. And Cynthia discovered Mitch had a network of three different physicians giving him pills. She put a stop to it, calling the doctors one by one and letting them know what was going on, informing Steve and Pappy that Mitch was using again. She told her husband to knock it off, or he'd be fired. And she meant it.

"Mitch has to remember he has partners," she says, head cocked defiantly. "And he doesn't get to write his own set of rules."

Is their relationship codependent? Even Cyn says the answer is certainly yes. But it's necessary. Mitch wouldn't function without her enabling. It's what he needs to manage his disease: steady control imposed by someone outside his own sparking, spiraling mind.

→

Bipolar disorder is not like diabetes. You can take your medication religiously—as Mitch does—yet still suffer symptoms. Psychiatrists are constantly refining and altering the cocktail, trying to come up with a magic potion that eliminates the illness without subtracting from the person. No one has ever gotten it exactly right.

"It's like one of those carnival games where you bop frogs with a mallet," Cynthia says. "The problem is over here, so you take a drug for that. Then it's changed, it's over here, and you need something new."

But there was a day a couple years into the marriage when she simply accepted this. He is, she says without sentiment, her whole heart. To be Mitch's wife means signing on for a lifetime of ups and downs, disappointments, frustration, and periodic bursts of anger at the stupid, potentially dangerous things he might do. She figures it's roughly a twentieth of their life together. Marriage to Mitch is nineteen parts dreamlike and one part nightmare.

And for a woman who *specifically* asked for someone who was "both sane and insane at the same time," those odds aren't bad . . .

music, and food. Even after all that, Mitch often forgets to file the actual marriage certificate afterward: three times, couples (including myself and my now-finally-legal husband) have

found out they weren't actually married at tax time, when their joint 1040 was bounced back by the IRS.

But what interests Mitch even more than weddings is rites for the dead. He's officiated at a few funerals and studied dozens of cultures' death mores, bringing together his interests in history, ritual, and the macabre. This is actually—oddly—how I ended up, one brilliant day in September 2006, standing in front of this man who had become like my brother, as he bound me (more or less) to my husband, my own midlife true love.

It started during the first week of 2006, a little over a year after I first walked into Hell's Kitchen and met Mitch. I'd quit my job at the magazine a few weeks before, after a series of disputes with management that culminated over a negative review. Then, with Mitch and Cyn's encouragement, I'd written a scathing tell-all about the food reviewing business for

Salon that disclosed every dishonest, elitist element—all the freebies and secret deals. "Food Slut" was a sensation, hotly controversial and my most-read essay to date. I was pretty sure my career as a critic was over. Mostly, I was glad.

But it was winter in Minnesota, and the days were dark. The holiday season was a ridiculous time to look for a job. The only thing I'd found locally was a temporary freelance gig with an alternative weekly—filling in for a writer who was on maternity leave—but they had no money for expenses, so I had to come up with ideas that cost nothing to write. Luckily, Mitch was in a manic phase, studying and talking nonstop about embalming techniques (often while he was slicing cold, raw meat). So I pitched a piece about funerals and showed up at his condo one night in late December to discuss. Mitch, of course, threw a party to mark the occasion and invited several friends.

One of them came from a tiny town called Montgomery, where the women at the American Legion Hall had been making the same "funeral hot dish" for ten years. I ended the evening with far more material than I needed, plus the name of the woman who developed the recipe, which, she would tell me on the phone the following day, served fifty and cost about thirty-five dollars to make.

But before I left, Cynthia pulled me aside and gave me a hug. "It's time for you to get online and find a man," she said as I put on my layers, preparing to go back out into the cold. "Just give it one more try."

I am not typically an obedient woman. But that night, after hours of wine and warm con-

American Legion Funeral Hot Dish

There are apparently people in Montgomery, Minnesota, who show up at every interment, whether they knew the deceased or not, just to get a helping of JoAnn Petricka's famous funeral hot dish.

5 pounds ground beef
1 large white onion, chopped (2 cups)
1 (16-ounce) bag frozen sliced carrots
1 (16-ounce) bag frozen cauliflower florets
1 (16-ounce) bag frozen broccoli florets
1 (50-ounce) can cream of mushroom soup
1 (50-ounce) can cream of chicken soup
1 bunch celery, chopped
¼ cup soy sauce
1 teaspoon white pepper
3 (12-ounce) bags chow mein noodles

Preheat oven to 325°F.

Fry hamburger and chopped onion in a large cast iron skillet, breaking ground beef into small pieces with a potato masher. Place beef and onions in a large roasting pan. Mix frozen vegetables, soups, chopped celery, soy sauce, and pepper in a very large bowl. Pour into the roasting pan, and blend with meat and onions. Fold in 2 bags of the chow mein noodles. Cover and bake 75 minutes. Remove the roasting pan from the oven. Sprinkle remaining bag of chow mein noodles on top. Put cover back on, and bake another 15 minutes. Serves 50.

versation with people who were happily and completely paired up, I thought, *What the hell?* I went straight home and logged onto an Internet dating site I'd used once before.

The first time had been a bust. I'd gone out with a handful of guys so completely wrong for me that halfway through the first date I would be aching to go home, put on my pajamas, and settle down in front of the TV. Mitch and Cynthia's story of inevitable, immediate love was freakish—never to be duplicated, especially by someone like me. I was, at that point, the unemployed, single mother of three teenagers, one with autism. A small, serious-looking Jewish woman in a land of leggy, blonde Swedes.

What's more, I'd failed miserably at my first marriage to a man remarkably like Mitch. The husband I married at twenty had been an addict and a big spender with bipolar tendencies. I stuck it out for thirteen years but couldn't, in the end, become the kind of wife Cyn had. Instead, I'd gotten dictatorial and bitter. Always before when she'd told me to look for my soul mate, I'd insisted it was hopeless. I was not wife or even steady girlfriend material and refused to make the same mistake again.

This is stupid, I thought that night, even as I typed my password, updated my profile, and entered parameters to search for suitable men.

The next day, I heard from a mathematician and weekend motorcycle racer named John. We corresponded for two weeks before meeting in person. A week after that, I took him to Hell's Kitchen and introduced him to my closest friends. He proposed in March, on the afternoon of my fortieth birthday, about a month

later. It was crazy. I called Mitch, who *knows* crazy. He told me real love and second chances are rare and I shouldn't fuck this up. Then he offered to marry us on his boat.

The wedding with a twenty-mile-per-hour wind: Mitch marrying Ann and John

When you are married by Mitch Omer, planning a wedding is literally a one-stop shopping experience. He is the minister, ship's captain, and executive chef. After pronouncing us man and wife, he and Cynthia brought out the simple, elegant menu he prepares for such occasions. Beef tenderloin, served rare on freshly made brioche. Jumbo shrimp with translucent tails. Grapes, Brie, Cristal. And a white cake with lemon curd—the only real nod to tradition—served with vanilla cream as lacy as a veil.

But more important than all that, it's being sanctified by Mitch's exuberant and profane brand of hope—the kind that comes from watching his parents still in love after sixty years, from seeing his brother marry at seventeen and die with his wife of three decades beside him, from finally meeting Cyn, the one woman who could handle and love and keep him, at the age of forty-six.

Brioche Bread

Brioche is the monarch of breads and lends itself to dozens of applications, from wrapping beef Wellington to the croutons we use for our salads. The bread is rich, with an excess of butter and eggs, and toasted it is unequaled in flavor.

5 tablespoons whole milk, divided

2 tablespoons granulated sugar

1 tablespoon active dry yeast

2½ cups all-purpose flour

4 teaspoons kosher salt, divided

5 large eggs at room temperature, well beaten

1 cup (2 sticks) unsalted butter, at room temperature

1 large egg yolk

Place 4 tablespoons of the milk and 2 tablespoons sugar in a small saucepan, and stir to mix well. Warm over low heat to 110°F. Pour into the bowl of a stand mixer, and sprinkle yeast over milk. Gently stir with a wooden spoon to mix. Let bloom, about 5 minutes.

Add flour, 2 teaspoons of the salt, and beaten eggs. With a dough hook, mix on low speed until dough is soft and moist, about 1 minute. Stop mixer, and scrape down the sides of the bowl. Continue mixing 1 minute.

Remove dough from the mixer, and turn out onto a well-floured surface. Knead until elastic, adding flour as necessary. Place in a large buttered bowl, turning to coat evenly with butter. Cover with a kitchen towel, and place in a warm area. Let rise until doubled, about 1½ hours. Remove from the bowl, punch down, turn over, cover, and let rest 11 minutes.

Return dough to the bowl of the stand mixer, and add 1 cup butter. Mix on medium speed with dough hook until butter is just incorporated, about 2 minutes. Turn out onto a well-floured surface, and knead to work in butter. Cover and let rest 10 minutes.

Flatten out dough with your hands on a lightly floured surface. Roll out dough to an 8 × 6–inch rectangle with a rolling pin, and then tightly roll up the rectangle of dough into an 8-inch log, pinching the seam together with your fingers. Grease an 8 × 4 × 2–inch bread pan with soft butter. Place dough log into the prepared pan, seam side down. Cover bread, and let rise until doubled, about 35 to 45 minutes.

Preheat oven to 425°F.

Combine egg yolk, 1 tablespoon of the milk, and 2 teaspoons of the salt in a small bowl, and whisk vigorously. Brush top of loaf with egg wash. Place the pan on the center rack of the oven, and bake until a glossy golden brown, about 47 to 59 minutes.

Turn loaf onto a wire rack, and let cool to room temperature. Wrap securely in plastic wrap. Can be refrigerated for up to 1 week or frozen for up to 6 months. Makes 1 loaf.

Grilled Jumbo Shrimp

20 raw U-6 to U-4 jumbo shrimp, peeled and deveined

1 cup Honey-Chipotle Sauce (see recipe)

Prepare Honey-Chipotle Sauce.

Mix shrimp and sauce in a large stainless steel, glass, or ceramic bowl, and place in a container with a tight-fitting lid. Cover and refrigerate 3 to 4 hours.

Prepare an outdoor grill with hot coals, and set a grill rack 4 inches from the coals (set heat to high if using a gas grill).

Grill shrimp undisturbed, until they begin to char slightly. Times will vary depending on the actual size of the shrimp you buy, so keep a close watch on them. Turn and continue cooking. The large shrimp that we use won't always cook through from the sides, so we finish by turning them on their backs. Eat *immediately*. Makes 4 servings.

HONEY-CHIPOTLE SAUCE

I've been using this recipe since 1990. But I recently found out it was more or less lifted from *The Thrill of the Grill*, by Chris Schlesinger and John Willoughby. It's a great book, which every chef who's even semiserious about barbecue should own.

½ cup honey

½ cup Rose's lime juice

1 (7-ounce) can chipotle peppers in adobo sauce

⅓ cup chopped fresh cilantro

¼ cup balsamic vinaigrette

¼ cup brown mustard

¼ cup peanut oil

4 medium cloves garlic, crushed

1 tablespoon ground black pepper

2 teaspoons kosher salt

Place all ingredients in a food processor fitted with a steel chopping blade, and pulse until well blended. Remove the lid, and scrape down the sides of the food processor with a rubber spatula. Return the lid, and purée the shit out of it. Pour sauce into a container with a tight-fitting lid. Will keep refrigerated for up to 1 month. Makes about 2½ cups.

Vanilla Buttermilk Layer Cake

3¾ cups cake flour, sifted

2½ cups granulated sugar

2 tablespoons baking powder

½ teaspoon kosher salt

1¼ cups (2½ sticks) butter, at room temperature

1¾ cups buttermilk, divided

3 eggs

4 egg yolks

1 tablespoon pure vanilla extract

Lemon or Key Lime Curd (see recipe)

Vanilla Whipped Cream (see recipe, p. 163)

Preheat oven to 325°F.

Combine flour, sugar, baking powder, and salt in the bowl of a stand mixer fitted with a paddle attachment. Pulse the mixer to sift ingredients. Stop mixer, and add butter in small chunks and 1¼ cup of the buttermilk. Mix on low speed to blend. Turn speed to medium, and mix until batter is light and fluffy, approximately 2 to 3 minutes.

Whisk together ½ cup of the buttermilk, eggs, egg yolks, and vanilla in a small bowl. Remove the bowl from the stand mixer, and fold in egg mixture in thirds.

Divide batter into 3 greased 9-inch layer pans, and place the pans on the center rack of the oven. Bake until edges are light golden brown, about 25 to 31 minutes. Remove the pans from the oven, and flip cake layers onto wire racks and let cool.

Prepare Lemon or Key Lime Curd and Vanilla Whipped Cream.

Spread the tops of two layers with lemon or key lime curd, and stack one layer on top of the other. Top cake with the final layer. Just before serving, spread vanilla whipped cream over top and sides of cake. Makes 8 to 10 servings.

LEMON OR KEY LIME CURD

1 cup granulated sugar

¾ cup fresh lemon or key lime juice

4 eggs

1½ cups (3 sticks) cold unsalted butter, cut into small chunks

Heat ½ cup of the sugar and juice to a boil in a small saucepan. Whisk eggs and remaining ½ cup of the sugar in a large stainless steel bowl. Temper the eggs by slowly adding hot juice mixture to egg mixture while whisking continually. Heat water to a simmer in a small saucepan. Place the bowl with egg mixture over it, still whisking continually, cooking until thickened to about the consistency of yogurt. Add butter chunks, and whisk until curd is shiny and smooth. Cover with plastic wrap, and cool immediately in a refrigerator. Makes about 2½ cups.

I n the evening of New Year's Day 2009—four days before the manuscript for this book was due—our families gathered: the one Mitch and Cynthia created and the one they helped me find. We sat around steaming fondue pots and talked until late. For once no one cooked anything elaborate, just melted cheese and bread, beef and sputtering oil. Our dessert was fresh fruit with chocolate. John and I shared a $7.99 bottle of wine.

"It's only food," Mitch often says. And he's right. I knew that back when I first met him, jaded by fancy restaurants and haughty chefs.

It's only food. But in the case of Hell's Kitchen, it's *not* only food, and that's the point. It's recipes from 1950s-era Des Moines. It's a mother's whimsy and a father's weekend breakfasts and the comfort of your favorite aunt. It's the color of rock and roll, the smell of an autumn afternoon in the woods, the taste of romance.

It's family. It's love. It's life.

New Year's Day 2009: Mitch, Cyn, Ann, and John

INDEX

alcoholic beverages
    Beer Margarita, 174
    Bloody Mary Mix, 172–73
    Kamikazes, Mitch and Steve's Oversize, 43
Anderson, Mark "Pappy," 53, 189
Angel Food Cake with Ginger-Tarragon Berries,
    162–63
Annie's Mustard, 12
antelope
    hunting, 188–89
    Stroganoff, 189
appetizers and snacks
    Chile-Cheese Squares, 13
    Cocktail Party Bean Dip, 12–13
    Curry Dip, 15
    Granola, 68
    Pretzels, Hot Damn Buttered, 168–69
    Salmon Tartare with Buttered Brioche Toast
        Points, 43–44
Atrium, 45
Aunt Fran's Chicken and Noodles, 24–26

bacon. *See also* BLTs
    on Nueske's thick-sliced applewood-smoked, 102
    in Rösti Potatoes, 64
    Salmon with Caramelized Shallots, Lemon,
        and, 41–42
    in Turkey Clubhouse Sandwich, 106
Bananas (steakhouse), 38
Bandy, Chris, 198
Bandy, Willow, 198
barbecue
    Beef Ribs, 138–39
    Pulled-Pork Sandwich, 112–14
    Ribs, Mitch's, 34–35

sauces
    Honey-Chipotle, 67
    Mitch's, 34–35
Bauer, Ann, 200–202, 206
beans, black
    Cocktail Party Bean Dip, 12–13
    Spicy, 66–67
bear
    hunting, 190
    Rib Roast of Bear, Bruce's, 190
beef. *See also* corned beef
    Barbecued Beef Ribs, 138–39
    French Dip, 114–15
Beer Margarita, 174
Beet Purée, 195
beverages. *See also* alcoholic beverages
    Cocoa, Hot Damn, 175
bipolar disorder, 47, 53, 199–200
Biscuits, 184
bison
    Benedict, 76
    Burger, 109–10
    Maple-Glazed Sausage, 73–74
    Sausage Bread, 58–59
blackberries
    in Ginger-Tarragon Berries, 163
    Jam, 144
Black Truffle Hollandaise Sauce, 156
Blinis, Jalapeño-Polenta with Sour Cream, Chives,
    and Caviar, 39
Bloody Mary Mix, 172–73
BLTs
    Mitch's Hellishly Good, 101–2
    Walleye, 104–5
    Walleye, Extra-Fancy, 191–92
blueberries, in Ginger-Tarragon Berries, 163

Bread Crumbs, Seasoned, 151
Bread Pudding, Brioche with Crème Anglaise, 164–65
breads
    Biscuits, 184
    Bison Sausage Bread, 58–59
    Brioche, 203–4
    Brioche Bread Pudding with Crème Anglaise,
       164–65
    brioche toast points, 43–44
    Caramel-Pecan Rolls, Dana's, 23–24
    Caraway Rye Bread, 117–18
    Pretzels, Hot Damn Buttered, 168–69
breakfast and brunch. *See also* eggs
    Bison Sausage Bread, 58–59
    Caramel-Pecan Rolls, Dana's, 23–24
    Corned Beef Hash, 89
    Crab Cakes, Steve's Tits-Up, 94–95
    French Toast, 63
    Frittatas, Individual Vegetable, 62
    Granola, 68
    Hash-Brown Potatoes, 63–64
    Huevos Rancheros, 65–66
    Mahnomin Porridge, 72–73
    Maple-Glazed Bison Sausage, 73–74
    oatmeal, 70–71
    pancakes, 68–70
    Rösti Potatoes, 64
    Syrup, Homemade, 72
brining
    corned beef, 91–92
    turkey breast, 107
Brioche Bread, 203–4
Brioche Bread Pudding with Crème Anglaise, 164–65
Brittle, Cookie, 166
broccoli, in Chicken Divan, 1960s-style, 19–21
Bruce's Rib Roast of Bear, 190
burgers. *See* hamburgers
butter
    Burnt, 186
    Clarified, 78
    Spiced, 101

cabbage
    Garlic Coleslaw, 15
    Great Napa Cabbage Salad, 16
    Sauerkraut, 119
Cabooze, Minneapolis, Minnesota, 35
cakes
    Angel Food with Ginger-Tarragon Berries, 162–63
    Vanilla Buttermilk Layer, 205
Caramel-Pecan Rolls, Dana's, 23–24
Caramel Sauce, 24
Caraway Rye Bread, 117–18
Caviar, Jalapeño-Polenta Blinis with Sour Cream,
    Chives, and, 39
Charred Chicken Breast Sandwich, 115–16
Charred Salmon with Pineapple-Jalapeño Salsa,
    193–94
Charred Sea Bass, 129–30
Charred Tuna with Beurre Noisette, 41
cheese
    Baked Rigatoni, 132–33
    Chile-Cheese Squares, 13
    Cocktail Party Bean Dip, 12–13
    Frittatas, Individual Vegetable, 62
    Grilled Cheese, Parmesan-Crusted, 98
    Ham and Pear Crisp, Hell's Kitchen, 100
    Huevos Rancheros, 65–67
    Jamaican Jerk Burger, 111–12
    Lasagna, Van Halen Style, 36–37
    Lemon-Ricotta Hotcakes, 80
    Lobster Tacos, 136
    Macaroni and Cheese, 131–32
    Morel Omelet à la Jacques Pépin, 180–81
    Mushroom-Crusted Shrimp Quiche, 182
    1960s-style Chicken Divan, 19–21
    Rueben Sandwich, 116–17
    Veggie and Cheese Panini, 120–22
chicken
    Aunt Fran's Chicken and Noodles, 24–26
    Divan, 1960s-style, 19–21
    Sandwich, Charred, 115–16
Chile-Cheese Squares, 13
chipotle peppers
    Honey-Chipotle Barbecue Sauce, 67
    Honey-Chipotle Sauce, 204
    in Salsa Con Misho, 146
chocolate
    Bunnies, 184–85
    Cookie Brittle, 166
    Fudge Sauce, 22–23

Hell's Kitchen Chocolate Chip and Peanut Butter
    Cookies, 166–67
Chocolate Chip and Peanut Butter Cookies, Hell's
    Kitchen, 166–67
Chutney, Lib's, 128–29
Clarified Butter, 78
Clubhouse Sandwich, Turkey, 106
Cocktail Party Bean Dip, 12–13
Cocoa, Hot Damn, 175
coconut, in Shrimp Lisabeth, 126–27
Coleslaw, Garlic, 15
condiments. See sauces and condiments
Cookie Brittle, 166
corned beef
    Hash, 89
    preparation, 91–92
    Rueben Sandwich, 116–17
Crab Cakes, Steve's Tits-Up, 94–95
Crawfish, Poached Halibut with Peas and, 44–45
Cream, Whipped, 23, 163
Crème Anglaise, 165
Curd, Lemon or Key Lime, 205
Curry Dip, 15
Curry Powder, Homemade Hot, 150

Dana's Caramel-Pecan Rolls, 23–24
deep-frying, 103
desserts
    Angel Food Cake with Ginger-Tarragon Berries,
        162–63
    Bread Pudding, Brioche with Crème Anglaise,
        164–65
    Cookie Brittle, 166
    Ice Cream Puffs, 21–23
    Peanut Butter and Chocolate Chip Cookies,
        Hell's Kitchen, 166–67
    toppings
        Caramel Sauce, 24
        Crème Anglaise, 165
        Fudge Sauce, 22–23
        Ginger-Tarragon Berries, 163
        Marshmallows, Homemade Miniature, 176–77
        Pecan Pieces, 24
        Whipped Cream, 23, 163
    Vanilla Buttermilk Layer Cake, 205

dips
    Cocktail Party Bean Dip, 12–13
    Curry Dip, 15
Dixon, Alexander, 38
Dry Jerk Seasoning, 149
Duluth, Minnesota, 52–53, 54

eggplant
    in Veggie and Cheese Panini, 120–22
    in Vegetable Benedict, 77
eggs
    about, 60–61
    benedict
        Bison, 76
        Mushroom, 78–79
        Nearly Classic, 74–75
        other variations, 79
        Vegetable, 77–78
    Fancy Fried Trout with Scrambled Eggs and Burnt
        Butter, 186
    Frittatas, Individual Vegetable, 62
    Huevos Rancheros, 65–66
    Morel Omelet à la Jacques Pépin, 180–81
    Scrambled with Lobster, 59–60

fish and seafood. See also lobster; salmon
    Crab Cakes, Steve's Tits-Up, 94–95
    Fish Fumet, 45
    Halibut with Peas and Crawfish, Poached, 44–45
    Jalapeño-Polenta Blinis with Sour Cream, Chives,
        and Caviar, 39
    Mushroom-Crusted Shrimp Quiche, 182
    Sea Bass, Charred, 129–30
    Shrimp Lisabeth, 126–27
    tartar sauces
        basic, 151
        Scallion-Jalapeño, 152
    Trout, Fancy Fried with Scrambled Eggs and Burnt
        Butter, 186
    Tuna with Beurre Noisette, Charred, 41
    Walleye BLT, 104–5
    Walleye BLT, Extra-Fancy, 191–92
French Dip, 114–15
French Toast, 63

Fried Morels, 181
Fried Oatmeal, 71
Frittatas, Individual Vegetable, 62
fruit. *See also* lemon; pineapple, golden
    Ginger-Tarragon Berries, 163
    Ham and Pear Crisp, Hell's Kitchen, 100
    jams and jellies
        Blackberry, 144
        Orange Marmalade, 145
    Ketchup from Hell, 142
    Lib's Chutney, 128–29
    Mahnomin Porridge, 72–73
    Tangerine-Jalapeño Hollandaise Sauce, 156
Fudge Sauce, 22–23
Funeral Hot Dish, American Legion, 201

Garlic Coleslaw, 15
Garlic Cream Sauce, 133
Gerdes, Cynthia, 49–53, 198, 199, 206
Gerdes, Katherine, 162
Ginger Purée, Sweetened, 173
Ginger-Tarragon Berries, 163
Goulash, Special Occasion, 19
Granola, 68
Graziano Brothers, Des Moines, Iowa, 135
Grilled Cheese, Parmesan-Crusted, 98
grilling
    Barbecue Ribs, Mitch's, 34–35
    Barbecued Beef Ribs, 138–39
    benedict
        Bison, 76
        Mushroom, 78–79
        Nearly Classic, 74–75
        Vegetable, 77–78
    Bison Burger, 109–10
    chicken, 115
    Chicken Breast Sandwich, Charred, 115–16
    Chocolate Bunnies, 184–85
    Jamaican Jerk Burger, 110
    Jumbo Shrimp, Grilled, 204
    Salmon, Charred with Pineapple-Jalapeño Salsa,
        193–94
    Sea Bass, Charred, 129
    Veggie and Cheese Panini, 120–22

Halibut with Peas and Crawfish, Poached, 44–45
ham
    Eggs Benedict, Nearly Classic, 74–75
    Mushroom Benedict, 78–79
    and Pear Crisp Sandwich, Hell's Kitchen, 100
hamburgers
    about, 110
    Bison, 109–10
    history of, 108
    Jamaican Jerk, 111–12
Hash-Brown Potatoes, 63–64
Hell's Kitchen openings
    Duluth, 52–53, 54
    Minneapolis, 50–53
hollandaise sauces
    Black Truffle, 156
    Lemon, 159
    Red Pepper, 154–55
    Sweet Cream, 153–54
    Sweet Pea, 158
    Tangerine-Jalapeño, 156
    Wild Mushroom, 157
Honey-Chipotle Barbecue Sauce, 67
Honey-Chipotle Sauce, 204
hotcakes. *See* pancakes and hotcakes
Hot Dish, American Legion Funeral, 201
Huevos Rancheros, 65–66

Ice Cream Puffs, 21–23
Italian Sausage, Hot, 134–35

jalapeño(s)
    -Pineapple Salsa, 130–31
    -Polenta Blinis with Sour Cream, Chives,
        and Caviar, 39
    -Tangerine Hollandaise Sauce, 156
    Tartar Sauce, Scallion-, 192
Jamaican jerk seasoning
    Burger, 111–12
    in Charred Salmon with Pineapple-Jalapeño
        Salsa, 193–94
    in Charred Sea Bass, 129
    Dry Jerk Seasoning, 149
    Wet Jerk Seasoning, 148–49

Jams and jellies
    Blackberry, 144
    Orange Marmalade, 145

Kamikazes, Mitch and Steve's Oversize, 43
Ketchup from Hell, 142
Key Lime Curd, 205

Lasagna, Van Halen Style, 36–37
Lasagna Noodles, Homemade, 37
lemon
    Curd, 205
    Hollandaise Sauce, 159
    Oil, 130
    Rice Pilaf, 194
    -Ricotta Hotcakes, 80
    Salmon with Caramelized Shallots, Lemon,
        and Bacon, 41–42
    Zest, Sweetened, 144
Lib's Chutney, 128–29
lobster
    boiled, 40
    Broth, 40
    Risotto with Roe and Fresh Peas, 39–40
    Scrambled Eggs with, 59–60
    Tacos, 136

Macaroni and Cheese, 131–32
Mahnomin Porridge, 72–73
Maple-Glazed Bison Sausage, 73–74
Margarita, Beer, 174
Marmalade, Orange, 145
Marshmallows, Homemade Miniature, 176–77
Mayonnaise, Homemade, 147
meats, USDA cooking recommendations, 73. *See also specific meats*
Meyer, Kim, 50
Meyer, Steve, 42–43, 46, 50
Mitch and Steve's Oversize Kamikazes, 43
Mitch's Barbecue Ribs, 34–35
Mitch's Hellishly Good BLT, 101–2
Mitch's Mashed Potatoes, 18
Mitch's World-Famous Peanut Butter, 143

mushrooms
    Benedict, 78–79
    Black Truffle Hollandaise Sauce, 156
    -Crusted Shrimp Quiche, 182
    morels
        Fried, 181
        hunting, 180
        Omelet à la Jacques Pépin, 180–81
        Quiche Shell with, 182
    in Veggie and Cheese Panini, 120–22
Mustard, Annie's, 12

Nagurski, Bronko, 12
Napa Cabbage Salad, Great, 16
Nearly Classic Eggs Benedict, 74–75
New French Café, Minneapolis, Minnesota, 38–43
1960s-style Chicken Divan, 19–21
Noodles, Egg, 18

oatmeal, 70–71
Oil, Lemon, 130
Omelet, Morel à la Jacques Pépin, 180–81
Omer, Annie, 9–12
Omer, Casey, 35, 38
Omer, Dana, 9–12, 45, 179–80, 183, 185, 187, 193
Omer, Jesse, 38, 198
Omer, Jill, 35, 38, 46
Omer, Lauren, 46
Omer, Libby, 10, 11
Omer, Mark, 10, 11
Omer, Mitch
    at Atrium, 45
    bipolar disorder, 47, 53, 199–200
    in California, 46
    childhood and family background, 9–12
    and Cynthia Gerdes, 49–50, 198, 199–200
    early adulthood, 33–34, 35
    in Ely, Minnesota, 33, 46–47
    holidays and celebrations, 197–98
    hunting and fishing, 179, 180, 182–83, 187, 190,
        191, 193
    marriages and funerals presided over, 198, 199,
        201–3
    at New French Café, 38, 42

at Pracna on Main, 42–43
signature, 99
and Steve Meyer, 42–43, 46
Orange Marmalade, 145

pancakes and hotcakes
Cornmeal, 70
Lemon-Ricotta Hotcakes, 80
Pancake Batter, Basic, 68–69
Pancake Batter Without Carbon's Malted Flour, 69
Panini, Veggie and Cheese, 120–22
pasta
Antelope Stroganoff, 189
Egg Noodles, 18
Goulash, Special Occasion, 19
Lasagna, Van Halen Style, 36–37
Lasagna Noodles, Homemade, 37
Macaroni and Cheese, 131–32
Rigatoni, Baked, 132–33
with Shrimp Lisabeth, 126–27
Spinach, 128
peanut butter
and Chocolate Chip Cookies, Hell's Kitchen, 166–67
Mitch's World-Famous, 143
Pear and Ham Crisp, Hell's Kitchen, 100
peas
Halibut with Peas and Crawfish, Poached, 44–45
Lobster Risotto with Roe and Fresh, 39–40
Sweet Pea Hollandaise Sauce, 158
Pecan Pieces, 24
peppadew peppers, in Salsa Con Misho, 146
peppers
chipotle
Honey-Chipotle Barbecue Sauce, 67
Honey-Chipotle Sauce, 204
in Salsa Con Misho, 146
jalapeño
-Pineapple Salsa, 130–31
-Polenta Blinis with Sour Cream, Chives, and Caviar, 39
-Tangerine Hollandaise Sauce, 156
Tartar Sauce, Scallion-Jalapeño, 192
peppadew
in Salsa Con Misho, 146

red
Hollandaise Sauce, 154
Roasted Red Pepper Purée, 155
in Vegetable Benedict, 77
Petricka, JoAnn, 201
Pickled Parrot, 46
pineapple, golden,
Jamaican Jerk Burger, 111–12
Pineapple-Jalapeño Salsa, 130–31
Salmon, Charred with Pineapple-Jalapeño Salsa, 193–94
Salsa con Misho, 146
polenta
Jalapeño-Polenta Blinis with Sour Cream, Chives, and Caviar, 39
in Salmon with Caramelized Shallots, Lemon, and Bacon, 41–42
Soft, 188
pork
Barbecue Ribs, Mitch's, 34–35
Pulled-Pork Sandwich, 112–14
Porridge, Mahnomin, 72–73
potatoes
Hash-Brown, 63–64
Mashed, Mitch's, 18
Rösti, 64
Pracna on Main, 42–45
Pretzels, Hot Damn Buttered, 168–69
Pulled-Pork Sandwich, Barbecued, 112–14
purées
Beet, 195
Ginger, Sweetened, 173
Roasted Red Pepper, 155

Quiche, Mushroom-Crusted Shrimp, 182

rabbit
Biscuits with Rabbit Gravy, 183–84
Chocolate Bunnies, 184–85
hunting, 182–83
red peppers
Hollandaise Sauce, 154
Roasted Red Pepper Purée, 155
in Vegetable Benedict, 77

ribs
  Barbecued Beef, 138–39
  Mitch's Barbecue, 34–35
  Rub, 150
rice
  Lobster Risotto with Roe and Fresh Peas, 39
  Mahnomin Porridge, 72–73
  Pilaf, Lemon, 194
Rigatoni, Baked, 132–33
Roasted Red Pepper Purée, 155
Rösti Potatoes, 64
Rub, Rib, 150
ruebens
  history of, 119
  Sandwich, 116–17
Rye Bread, Caraway, 117–18

salad dressing, Thousand Island, 118
salads
  Garlic Coleslaw, 15
  Great Napa Cabbage Salad, 16
salmon
  Charred with Pineapple-Jalapeño Salsa, 193–94
  Crispy with Caramelized Shallots, Lemon, and
    Bacon, 41–42
  Elise, 194–95
  fishing, 193
  Tartare with Buttered Brioche Toast Points, 43–44
salsa
  Con Misho, 146
  Pineapple-Jalapeño, 130–31
  Tomatilla, 137
saltpeter, 93
sandwiches. See also BLTs; hamburgers
  Chicken Breast, Charred, 115–16
  cutting and plating, 102
  French Dip, 114–15
  Ham and Pear Crisp, Hell's Kitchen, 100
  Parmesan-Crusted Grilled Cheese, 98
  Rueben, 116–17
  Turkey Clubhouse, 106–7
  Veggie and Cheese Panini, 120–22
sauces and condiments. See also hollandaise sauces;
    salsa

barbecue
  Honey-Chipotle, 67
  Mitch's, 34–35, 67
Caramel Sauce, 24
Chutney, Lib's, 128–29
Fudge Sauce, 22–23
Garlic Cream Sauce, 133
Honey-Chipotle Sauce, 204
jams and jellies
  Blackberry, 144
  Orange Marmalade, 145
Ketchup from Hell, 142
Lemon Zest, Sweetened, 144
Mayonnaise, Homemade, 147
Mustard, Annie's, 12
Peanut Butter, Mitch's World-Famous, 143
Steak Sauce, Homemade, 152
tartar sauces
  basic, 151
  Scallion-Jalapeño, 192
Tomato–Red Pepper Sauce with Hot Italian
    Sausage, 36–37
Velouté Sauce, 134
sauerkraut
  recipe, 119
  in Rueben Sandwich, 116–17
sausage
  Bison Sausage Bread, 58–59
  Goulash, Special Occasion, 19
  from Iowa, 135
  Italian, Hot, 134–35
  Maple-Glazed Bison, 73–74
  Tomato–Red Pepper Sauce with Hot Italian, 36–37
Scallion-Jalapeño Tartar Sauce, 192
Scrambled Eggs with Lobster, 59–60
Sea Bass, Charred, 129–30
seafood. See fish and seafood
shallots, Salmon with Caramelized Shallots, Lemon,
    and Bacon, 41–42
shrimp
  Grilled Jumbo, 204
  Lisabeth, 126–27
  Mushroom-Crusted Shrimp Quiche, 182
  size, 127
snacks. See appetizers and snacks

soups, stews, and stocks
    Chicken and Noodles, Aunt Fran's, 24–26
    Fish Fumet, 45
    Lobster Broth, 40
    Velouté Sauce as base for, 134
Spiced Butter, 101
spices and seasonings
    Curry Powder, Homemade Hot, 150
    Jamaican Jerk, 148–49
    Rib Rub, 150
Spicy Black Beans, 66–67
Spinach Pasta, 128
Steak Sauce, Homemade, 152
Steve's Tits-Up Crab Cakes, 94–95
strawberries, in Ginger-Tarragon Berries, 163
Stroganoff, Antelope, 189
Sugar, Vanilla, 175
Sweet Cream Hollandaise Sauce, 153–54
Sweet Pea Hollandaise Sauce, 158
Syrup, Homemade, 72
Szathmary, Louis, 99

Tacos, Lobster, 136
Tangerine-Jalapeño Hollandaise Sauce, 156
tartar sauces
    basic, 151
    Scallion-Jalapeño, 192
Thousand Island Dressing, 118
Tomatilla Salsa, 137
tomatoes. *See also* BLTs
    –Red Pepper Sauce with Hot Italian Sausage,
        36–37
    in Turkey Clubhouse Sandwich, 106
    in Vegetable Benedict, 77
    in Veggie and Cheese Panini, 121–23
Trout
    Fancy Fried with Scrambled Eggs and Burnt
        Butter, 186
    fishing, 185
Tuna with Beurre Noisette, Charred, 41
Turkey
    Baked Brined, 107
    Clubhouse Sandwich, 106

Vanilla Buttermilk Layer Cake, 205
Vanilla Extract, Homemade, 23
Vanilla Sugar, 175
vegetables. *See also specific vegetables*
    Benedict, 77–78
    and Cheese Panini, 120–22
    Curry Dip, 15
    Frittatas, Individual Vegetable, 62
Velouté Sauce, 134
venison
    hunting, 187
    Roasted with Root Vegetables over Soft Polenta,
        187–88

walleye
    BLT, 104–5
    BLT, Extra-Fancy, 191–92
    fishing, 191
Wet Jerk Seasoning, 148–49
Whipped Cream, 23, 163
wild game
    Antelope Stroganoff, 189
    Bear, Bruce's Rib Roast of, 190
    rabbit
        Biscuits with Rabbit Gravy, 183–84
        Chocolate Bunnies, 184–85
    Venison, Roasted with Root Vegetables over Soft
        Polenta, 187–88
Wild Mushroom Hollandaise Sauce, 157

Picture Credits

Damn Good Food was designed and set in type by Percolator Graphic Design, Minneapolis. The main typeface is Absara, designed by Xavier Dupré. Printed by Transcontinental Printing.